Social Pedagogy in the UK

Theory and Practice

Kieron Hatton

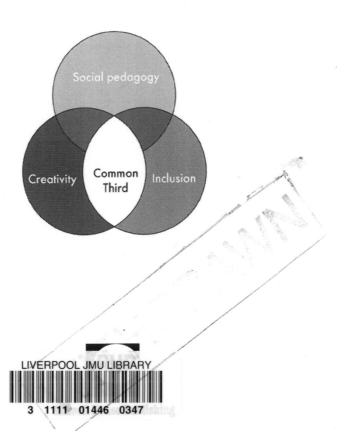

First published in 2013 by:
Russell House Publishing Ltd.
58 Broad Street
Lyme Regis
Dorset DT7 3QF

Tel: 01297-443948
Fax: 01297-442722
e-mail: help@russellhouse.co.uk
www.russellhouse.co.uk

British Library Cataloguing-in-publication Data:
A catalogue record for this book is available from the British Library.

ISBN: 978-1-905541-89-8

Typeset by TW Typesetting, Plymouth, Devon

Printed by IQ Laser Press, Aldershot

About Russell House Publishing

Russell House Publishing aims to publish innovative and valuable materials to help managers, practitioners, trainers, educators and students.

Our full catalogue covers: families, children and young people; engagement and inclusion; drink, drugs and mental health; textbooks in youth work and social work; workforce development.

Full details can be found at www.russellhouse.co.uk and we are pleased to send out information to you by post. Our contact details are on this page. We are always keen to receive feedback on publications and new ideas for future projects.

Contents

About the Author

Kieron Hatton is Professional Lead Social Work at Portsmouth University. He has extensive experience of developing and delivering programmes in European Social Work, in conjunction with partners in a number of countries including Denmark, Germany, Finland, Norway, France, Spain, Poland, Hungary and the Czech Republic. He has a wide range of experience of working in, experiencing and delivering educational programmes in social care and child care; and has worked with local and national agencies to develop training in social pedagogy for staff working with services for young people in the Looked After Care system, and adolescents with mental health problems. Prior to joining the university he worked in the voluntary and community sectors and was closely involved in campaigns against benefits cuts, the promotion of Travellers rights and housing campaigns across south Wales.

Acknowledgements

Helen, Cal and Ruari for their support.

Ruari for his administrative help.

Members of the School of Health Sciences and Social Work at the University of Portsmouth, particularly Annabel, Graham and Assaf, who acted as readers/advisers.

All the students and academic colleagues from the UK and Europe who helped develop the ideas in this book.

Those students who contributed to Chapter 6.

Introduction

Social pedagogy is an approach to service delivery which is common across Europe and which is attracting increasing interest in the United Kingdom. It is an approach used with a wide variety of people: those with disabilities, children in residential services, young people involved in criminal justice, people who are homeless, people misusing substances, adults, and with women and community groups. It has three key elements, which it is arguable, have been lost from much of the welfare practice in this country:

1. A focus on the importance of relationships, particularly those based on equality, partnership and inclusion.
2. An approach to practice which promotes 'risk' taking.
3. A focus on the person as a whole, who is influenced by, and influences, the environment around them, be that at the level of family/personal relationship, community and prevailing culture or the wider social and economic environment.

Hämäläinen (2003: 76) suggests that 'the basic idea of social pedagogy is to promote people's social functioning, inclusion, participation, social identity and social competence as members of society'. The Social Pedagogy Development Network defines social pedagogy as an:

> ... academic discipline that draws on core theories from various related disciplines, such as education, sociology, psychology and philosophy. In essence, it is concerned with well-being, learning and growth. This is underpinned by humanistic values and principles which view people as active and resourceful agents, highlight the importance of including them into the wider community, and aim to tackle or prevent social problems and inequality.
>
> Social Pedagogy Development Network downloaded from
> www.thempra.org.uk/social pedagogy.htm on 1/11/12

These foci on inclusion, social functioning and social competence and on influencing the environment in which people using services live have led to a growing interest in the efficacy of social pedagogy as a model and method of social intervention. As such social pedagogy has gained currency in the UK over the last ten years.

The election of the Coalition government in May 2010 presaged significant challenges to the work of social workers, youth workers, community workers and other welfare professionals. Strangely, despite the context of austerity within which these changes were framed, the changes presented opportunities as well as challenges. The deregulation of much state activity lessened the controls placed on the actions of such professionals and the 'Big Society' agenda provided space (if within the context of considerably reduced resources) for welfare professionals to use the language of social action, community and empowerment to reclaim a more positive approach to our work (for a fuller discussion of how these changes can be used to support a more progressive agenda see below). Jordan (2011: 13) has suggested that this agenda was a specific response to what he called the 'very technocratic, formal, managerial and economistic approach ... to influence individual behaviour' characteristic of New Labour. He suggests that it offers an escape from New Labour's mechanistic views of human behaviour and opportunities because of its focus on action.

It is within this context that attention has focused on different ways of delivering welfare services. These include *Reclaiming Social Work* (the Hackney model), the outcomes of the Social Work Reform Board and Munro, the personalisation and co-production agendas in adult social care, the challenges of the new agendas in youth and community work and the promotion of local agendas allegedly more sensitive to local needs (localism). Within this challenging, and fast changing, environment attention has focused on how we can deliver our services differently, and, if we are to deliver them differently, what we can learn from the way other countries deliver their services. This has come at an opportune time for those who have felt for some time that the UK could learn from the European tradition of social pedagogy (Higham, 2001; Hatton, 2006, 2008; Cameron et al., 2011; the Social Pedagogy Development Network – SPDN, 2012).

Behind this increasing interest in social pedagogy lie a number of important influences which include:

- An increasing interest in international and European models of social intervention (Lorenz, 1994; Lyons, 1999; Healy, 2001; Lyons and Lawrence, 2006; Petrie et al., 2006; Hatton, 2008).
- The development of a number of degree level courses in higher education which offered social pedagogy as part of its curricula – BA (Hons) Curative Education at the University of Aberdeen, BA (Hons) European Social Work and Social Care at the University of Portsmouth, BA (Hons) Social Pedagogy and Social Care at Liverpool Hope University, the MA Social Pedagogy at the Institute of Education in the University of London.
- Research carried out in the UK looking at the efficacy of social pedagogy in meeting the needs of young people in residential care. The central drivers for this work were the National Centre for Excellence in Residential Child Care (NCERCC), the National

Children's Bureau, the Social Education Trust and the Thomas Coram Research Unit at the Institute of Education in the University of London.

The development of an international perspective in social and community work has a long history. Kendall (2000) pointed to the hundred years' history of social work education in the US and in associated developments in the UK. She notes the continuing relevance of social work to the amelioration of the complex social problems contemporary society faces when she says:

> *The problems with social, economic and human relationships with which social workers deal will continue to require a broad understanding of human behaviour in all its aspects, together with knowledge of the social, economic, and political institutions that constitute the context for social work practice.*
>
> Kendall, 2000: 108

A similar point is made by Lyons and Lawrence (2006) when they note the importance of the cross-national development of the social professions and the way in which global factors play an increasingly important part in the way that those professions deal with a complex array of social issues. As I have noted elsewhere one of the challenges for social workers is to 'learn from each other; to reject national specifications of their role and to embrace the knowledge, skills and experiences of other countries' (Hatton, 2006: 105).

Writers such as Hugman (2010) and Lavalette and Ferguson (2007) have pointed to the way an international perspective can allow us to see how local and global perspectives can enrich our practice and how traditions from very different countries can be utilised to create or recreate progressive forms of practice. This book will draw on a wide range of writers within the literature from Che Guevara to Freire to Vygotsky to illustrate how we can reconstitute our practice. To allow us to do this the book will focus on a wide range of professions – social work, community development, youth work, work with people with disabilities, and adult social care – and to facilitate the discussion I will use the phrase 'social professions' to characterise the people for whom this book may have a relevance.

The phrase 'social professionals' will be used in the way proposed by Lorenz (1998: 123) to include, 'social pedagogues, social and special educators, agogues, animateurs, social workers, youth workers and community workers'. Further, Marynowicz-Hetka, Piekarski and Wagner (1999: 23) suggest that:

> . . . *the category of social professions includes both professionals, that is persons specially trained to work with specific types of persons, families, social groups and communities at high social risk, as well as persons who conduct this type of work as volunteers and have no professional training.*

In preparing the book I have also spoken to people from other professions who have indicated that they believe the concept of social pedagogy could contribute to new agendas in a range of other professions including complementary medicine, occupational therapy, speech and language therapy, criminal justice, education, psychology and mental health services. The international nature of the debates within social pedagogy can make a contribution to the development of a range of health and social care practices.

Two examples illustrate this point:

- The author ran a briefing session for a mental health trust in the south east of England. The briefing was attended by social workers, psychologists and assistant psychologists, mental health nurses and occupational therapists. The response of the participants was enthusiastic and the various professionals all indicated that social pedagogy could be used in their practice to improve outcomes for the people they worked with.
- The University of Portsmouth ran a conference on Participatory Arts and Social Practices in 2011 with artists from across the South of England (community and gallery based) who were engaged with local communities to promote the empowerment, through art, of those communities. A core presentation was around creativity and social pedagogy and its relevance to promoting inclusive agendas.

These issues form core themes throughout the book.

Beyond Children's Services: Alcohol and Narcotics Anonymous (ANA) Portsmouth

As mentioned in the preceding discussion social pedagogy has the potential to improve the delivery of services across a range of sectors. The author has explored its potential in a number of the ways described above. An interesting possible development is in the field of substance misuse, where practitioners often use a variety of techniques to encourage people to reflect on their experience and motivations for change; individual counselling; group or house meetings; engagement with the wider community etc.

ANA is a well established agency which seeks to support people to confront their dependency through a range of techniques. Recently students from the social work programmes at the University of Portsmouth (see Chapter 2) undertook a presentation to the staff group about social pedagogy. The staff immediately saw the connection with their own approach and social pedagogy and are now incorporating a social pedagogic approach, particularly the emphasis on groupwork, relationship building and the idea of the common third, into their work. They are currently rewriting their mission statement to clearly articulate their commitment to social pedagogy as an approach to substance misuse.

Libby Reid, Director of ANA says:

Our engagement with social pedagogy has given us the language and the theoretical underpinning to place our work in a wider context of social practice.

A Brief Outline of the Book's Structure

Part One discusses the development of social pedagogy as an academic discipline and its influence on UK debates about welfare practice.

Part Two develops the theoretical structure within which an understanding of the potential of social pedagogy in UK welfare practice can be understood. Chapter 1 describes the development of social pedagogy and Chapter 2 looks at some of the key thinkers behind our understanding of what social pedagogy is. Chapters 3 and 4 provide a theoretical framework for understanding how key ideas from within social pedagogy can be linked to notions of inclusion and creativity to provide a conceptual model for understanding social pedagogy. However, the discussion in Chapter 5 highlights how, for such a conception to take forward the debate, it needs to be linked to an awareness of how power relations impact on the social pedagogic relationship.

Part Three focuses on practice situations within which social pedagogy can be seen to be effective. Beginning in Chapter 6 with the experience of social pedagogic students studying at the University of Portsmouth, it describes how they experienced learning about UK social care and applied their own experiential models to investigate how their own countries and UK services could benefit from a better mutual understanding of what each other does. Chapter 7 looks at the lessons to learned from attempts to introduce social pedagogy into children's residential services in the UK: much of this material may already be familiar to students of social pedagogy. This chapter is followed by discussions of how social pedagogy can contribute to other areas of practice including youth work, adult social care and community development.

Part Four looks at the challenge social pedagogy poses to the UK, particularly in the light of the outcomes of the Munro Review and the work of the Social Work Task Force, the Social Work Reform Board and social work's transfer to a new regulator – the Health and Care Professions Council. It asks if it is possible to develop a UK social pedagogy.

Part Five, concludes with some initial thoughts on how the relationship focus of much of the discussion of social pedagogy can be fused with a broader analysis of social pedagogy's potential to promote social change to create a 'structural social pedagogy'. The book ends with a following a guide to further reading and a list of useful organisations and addresses.

Part One: The Context

Chapter 1: The Development of Social Pedagogy in the UK

The penetration of social pedagogy into UK higher education

There has been a progressive development of social pedagogy as an academic discipline within higher education within the UK over the last ten to fifteen years. Initially these developments had a primarily educational focus. It was part of an overall internationalisation of the curricula which was occurring at that time (Van Der Wende, 2001). However there has been an increase in interest in learning from international models and applying them to improve practice (Lyons, 1999; Hatton, 2006). This chapter will look at the ensuing influence on UK debates about the education of social professionals and the implications for welfare practice.

While there are a limited number of courses in the UK offering social pedagogy as a subject of study – currently the BA (Hons) Social Pedagogy (previously the BA (Hons) Curative Education) at Aberdeen University, the BA (Hons) Social Care and Social Pedagogy at Liverpool Hope, the Certificate in Higher Education in Social Pedagogy at University Campus Suffolk and the MA Social Pedagogy at the Institute of Education – a number of courses utilise social pedagogic approaches across their curriculum. The University of Portsmouth has mainstreamed social pedagogy across its social work curriculum.

Hessle (2002) questioned whether social pedagogy had a role in higher education as part of the introductory address to the FESET congress in Stockholm in 2001. He confessed pessimism about the ability of social pedagogy to maintain a professional profile, certainly within the Swedish higher education system. The author does not believe that this pessimistic evaluation is borne out by developments within the UK. The BA in Curative Education (BA in Social Pedagogy since 2010) which was introduced as a partnership between Camphill Ruldolf Steiner Schools and the University of Aberdeen in 2003 was an attempt to develop an approach to training residential workers which was based on social pedagogic principles (Jackson, 2003). Smith and White (2008) have argued that social pedagogy is consistent and resonant with Scottish approaches to social welfare. They see social pedagogy as a way of promoting new forms of social work intervention which promote social well being.

The University of Portsmouth ran a BA (Hons) European Social Work and Social Care (BAESW) from 1992 to 2007 and an MA European Social Work from 1998 to 2002. The philosophy of the MA was based on:

. . . the increasing influence of European (as opposed to individual state) legislation, directives and initiatives in the social areas of life. Examples of this influence are found in EU statements and policies in such spheres as disability, childcare, gender equality and, more generally, social exclusion – all areas where from time to time welfare professionals may be involved.

It is considered important for such professionals to consider the differing national ethical and value bases underpinning their work; to understand their histories, welfare state structures and the current variety of systems of service delivery within Europe. The development and use of the analytical skills required will assist professional competence, and encourage reflective practice. Additionally there will be opportunities for students to compare working methods across the Union in an attempt to develop best practice and procedures.

MA European Social Work, Course Handbook, 2000/1

Both courses were based firmly around social pedagogic principles, the BA was taught jointly with Skovtovte Socialpedagogic Seminarium in Copenhagen and latterly with Froebel Seminariet also in Copenhagen. The course sought to integrate UK and Danish perspectives on social work and social pedagogy and as such adopted a range of approaches to education including group work between students from Denmark, Norway, the UK, Germany, Spain and a number of other countries. As Hatton (2006: 120) noted, the course was based on educational principles through which 'the students are expected to use a wide range of creative and artistic skills, both to facilitate their learning and in their final presentations'. Hatton (2006: 124) pointed to the way in which such a programme can provide an:

. . . in depth understanding of the importance of different histories, social policies and value systems (which) can help us meet the needs of undergraduate students who are seeking to expand their horizons beyond their country of origin.

In Portsmouth, the BAESW was based on the concept of students using a mixture of traditional educational methods and artistic and creative methods. The programme was taught jointly in Portsmouth and with Froebel Seminariet in Copenhagen. A key element of the Copenhagen part of the programme was the use of a wide range of creative and artistic skills to facilitate learning and as part of the group presentations. As Hatton (2006: 120) notes:

. . . students spend a period during each week developing this side of their skills repertoire, whether it be learning a musical instrument, learning a practical skill or engaging in drama. Such an approach is central to the idea of 'common third' where the social worker/pedagogue and the service user are each expected to

bring something to their relationship so that they can create something together equally.

These courses are now closed, however the University of Portsmouth has mainstreamed social pedagogy into its core social work curriculum. A key idea, the 'common third' (see Chapter 3) is operationalised in this context by developing an international focus within the curricula, fusing this with an inclusion perspective and underpinning this with a focus on creativity. An example is the *Creativity and Empowerment* unit in which the students are expected to work with service users/carers to produce a creative artefact – film, music, drama, poetry, sculpture. The philosophy is based on the 'common third' and the students are assessed on their ability to engage and work with the service users/carers rather than the quality of the artefact they produce. This unit is highly valued by all the participants and is reflected both on the service user website (www.swig.uk.net) and the social work programme area website (www.particip8.port.ac.uk).

Liverpool Hope University introduced a BA in Social Care and Social Pedagogy in 2007. Their course is based on an attempt to show the relevance of social pedagogy to social care practice. It provides a pathway for people who wish to undertake a qualification outside of the traditional social work education qualification. It includes units on Social Pedagogy and Social Care in Practice, a social pedagogy case study and reflective essays along with units demonstrating the link between social pedagogy and social care in the UK. Within the Liverpool Hope programme students are taught using a mixture of traditional methods and creative experiences.

The degree included a wide range of field practice that gave students the opportunity to work with individuals, groups and communities. Selective projects that students engaged with were: planning and implementing a dating violence prevention project in the University; planning a Living Library in the community of Toxteth; befriending people with dementia. The dating violence prevention project included developing and disseminating relevant educational material (posters and fliers), setting up educational stalls, networking with community organisations, developing a small theatrical happening etc. In the Living Library project members of the community who have experience of a range of social issues engaged in discussion and debate with other members of the community about their experience (information provided in correspondence with the author by Maria Pentaraki, Programme Leader for The Social Pedagogy Degree Programme, Liverpool Hope University).

The BA in Curative Education at the University of Aberdeen commenced in March 2003 and was recognised as an appropriate qualification for people working in the Scottish residential childcare sector by the Scottish Social Services Council. Jackson has described curative education as 'a multi disciplinary professional activity in which aspects of care, education, therapeutic and medical activities, the use of crafts and creative arts are integrated to form a holistic approach in supporting children and adults with complex needs' (p. 65). The degree is provided in partnership with the Camphill movement which operates on principles laid down by Rudolph Steiner. Jackson suggests that social pedagogy could add an important and positive focus to the future of residential children's services. He noted that the introduction of social pedagogy would:

> *Necessitate not only a radical transformation in the character of residential care but also fundamental changes in the nature and purpose of professional training for those working in child care services.*
>
> Jackson, 2006: 62–3 (see discussion in Chapter 6)

This programme has now been revalidated as the BA in Social Pedagogy and remains accredited by the Scottish Social Services Council. The Course descriptor says that the professional training in social pedagogy encompasses the following:

- A sound knowledge of the holistic understanding of the human being.
- An understanding of human life course development.
- An understanding of general social pedagogical principles, theories and approaches.
- An ever-expanding repertoire of practical social pedagogical attitudes, skills and methods.
- Social and organisational skills to facilitate working in and building community.
- The ability to work within the professional, social-political and regulatory context of the field.
- The ability to work in partnership with parents, carers, colleagues and other professionals.
- The ability to develop trusting and positive relationships.
- The creative ability to develop new ideas for transformative action.
- Personal and professional development.

The programme clearly draws on key pedagogic principles of focusing on positive relationships, the development of theoretical knowledge, practical skills and creative abilities.

From September 2013 the Institute of Education at the University of London are offering the MA Social Pedagogy: Working with Children and Families whose purpose is described as to:

- Introduce you to the field of social pedagogy, its concepts and principles, and current theories about social pedagogic ways of working with children.

- Critically explore the life circumstances of children, including those in public care, and the implications for professional practice with children.
- Investigate new ways of understanding communication and interpersonal relationships.

Hallstedt and Högström reviewed social work curricula in the Netherlands, Norway and Ireland. They sought to demonstrate how social pedagogic approaches can be found in a variety of field work contexts. They describe an Irish community work setting, a welfare nurse in another part of Europe, and an institution for people with learning difficulties in Amsterdam. They suggest that social pedagogical activities 'are based on help and assistance to people in need. The activities are emancipating, aiming at mobilisation of human resources. The activities are also pedagogical interventions imbued by power, since one person seeks to influence another' (Hallstedt and Högström, 2005: 13–14).

Hallstedt and Högström suggest that at the core of a social pedagogic curriculum are three basic elements:

1. There is an equality in the relationship between the student and the service user/client.
2. There is a strong emphasis on goal directed work.
3. Social pedagogic education has a significant amount of non-traditional elements within it. There is a particular stress on 'artistic methods (which) promote self reflection as a strong asset in the social educational worker' (p. 270).

This element of creativity is central to the programmes described above and is a key element of social pedagogy (see Chapter 4).

The developing interest in social pedagogy in the UK

The first significant mention of social pedagogy in the UK comes in a collection from the Federation Internationale Des Communautés Educatives (FICE) produced in 1984 and edited by Davies Jones, one of the first UK social work academics to demonstrate an interest in social pedagogy. He noted how social pedagogy's initial focus is around residential childcare but pointed out that pedagogues also worked with people with disabilities, in therapeutic relationships and in crisis intervention. He pointed to the way in which pedagogues also worked in nursery, day care, pre-school and with young people in the community. He showed how pedagogues worked with older people and people in the criminal justice system. He argued that it was essential for pedagogues to work in collaboration with other professionals.

The Thomas Coram Research Unit (TCRU) has been conducting research since 2000 which has aimed to examine the ways in which European models of social pedagogy can be applied to English residential care. In a preliminary study in 2007 they pointed to four studies which they had undertaken between 2000 and 2007 which looked at the issues raised by social pedagogy by focusing in particular on pedagogic activity in Denmark and Germany with reference also to social pedagogy in other European countries including France and Holland. The four studies were as follows:

- The first study for the Department of Health TCRU looked at what was understood by pedagogy, its common characteristics and the training peculiar to social pedagogues. They drew attention in particular to the pedagogue's focus on the child's 'associative life', in particular the way pedagogues share the children's life space and drew attention to the pedagogue's focus on everyday activities such as eating together, homework, play and creative activities.

- The second study (for DH/DfES) compared residential services for children in England with those found in Denmark and Germany. They noted that pedagogues in Denmark held a higher level of qualification and they noted that English workers 'referred more frequently to procedural or organisational matters and to short term behaviour management, indicating a less professional role then that adopted by pedagogues' (Cameron, McQuail and Petrie, 2007:26). Young people in England also reported less satisfaction with the way decisions were made in their units and greater concern with staff turnover, recruitment and retention.

- The third study looked at foster care in Demark, France, Germany and Sweden. They noted that there were not many foster carers qualified as pedagogues but that in Europe they were more frequently trained by pedagogues (see Chapter 6 and Cameron and Petrie, 2011).

- The fourth study in 2006, funded by the Esmée Fairbairn Foundation, identified a number of existing courses which adopted social pedagogic principles in the UK (see above), a number of therapeutic communities including Camphill, Steiner and Montessori schools which were operated on pedagogic principles, and examined the work of social pedagogic students working in the UK.

A key element of the approaches adopted by the pedagogues that TCRU studied was an emphasis on creative activities. TCRU was at this stage sceptical about the possibility of including such activities in the UK as the training of residential workers lacked such a focus. However we will see in Chapter 3 that such initiatives have a place in UK education. The TCRU position on this now appears to more responsive to the possibilities of introducing such a creative approach (Petrie and Chambers, 2009).

In a briefing paper from 2009, TCRU identified the following key principles of pedagogic practice (Petrie et al., 2009: 4):

- A focus on the child as a whole person, and support for the child's overall development.

- A practitioner seeing herself/himself as a person, in relationship with the child or young person.
- While they are together, children and staff are seen as inhabiting the same life space, not as existing in separate, hierarchical domains.
- As professionals, pedagogues are encouraged to constantly reflect on their practice and to apply both theoretical understandings and self knowledge to their work and to the sometimes challenging demands with which they are confronted.
- Pedagogues should be both practical and creative; their training prepares them to share in many aspects of children's daily lives, such as preparing meals and snacks or making music and building kites.
- In group settings, children's associative life is seen as an important resource: workers should foster and make use of the group.
- Pedagogy builds on an understanding of children's rights that is not limited to procedural matters or legislative requirements.
- There is an emphasis on teamwork and valuing the contribution of others – family members, other professionals and members of the local community – in the task of 'bringing up' children.

Petrie et al. (2009: 7) argue that pedagogy has much to offer children and parents in the UK. In particular they suggest that it is inclusive, child focused rather than procedure focused, focuses on the individual child and the groups to which they belong and that their creative work may, 'enhance children's self esteem and . . . be therapeutic, in the wider sense of that word'.

Petrie and Statham (2009) noted that in France the profession closest to pedagogy, education specialise, was more 'practical than that of the social worker. It was about *doing*, and doing *with* someone ('C'est le faire avec') and about working with relationships ('travailler avec des relations')'. (Petrie and Statham, 2009: 8). Ott, a French social pedagogue said at a recent conference, 'I use the framework of social pedagogy as a source of inspiration. We are influenced by Paulo Freire, Korczak and Freinet . . . we are interested in the children not the school . . . (however) . . . we analyse also the institutions' (2012). Elsewhere he has also suggested that social pedagogic influences can be found in the work of Sartre, Rousseau and Aristotle and that the role of the social pedagogue involves a combination of transmitting ideas, transforming society and education (p. 26) (Ott, 2011: 66–7).

Petrie and Statham point to a clear distinction in professional roles between social workers and social pedagogues in Germany and suggest that often the social pedagogic qualification was seen as a lower level, foundation type qualification, for social workers wishing to enter into work with children and families.

NCERCC (National Centre for Excellence in Residential Child Care) and SET (the

Social Education Trust) undertook a pilot study testing out the efficacy of social pedagogy in a small number of residential units in the north west and south east of the UK (Bengtsson et al., 2008). The study identified a number of benefits emanating from the project, including the fact that 2/3rds of the participants reported an increase in their understanding of social pedagogy; that it helped them improve their skills in working with young people; and that they felt inspired to use social pedagogy in their practice. They noted in particular the importance of 'management buy in' to the introduction of social pedagogy to any agency (pp. 20–3).

In 2008 TCRU were commissioned by the DCSF/DH to undertake a pilot project to assess whether or not social pedagogy could make a useful contribution to the improvement of children's residential services in the UK. The research was commissioned as a result of developments around *Every Child Matters* (DfES, 2003) and *The Children's Plan* (DCSF, 2007). Following this the *Children and Young People's Workforce Strategy* (DCSF, 2008) suggested the development of a Youth Professional Status which should be underpinned by a social pedagogic approach. Details of the project design can be found in *Briefing Paper 2*, February 2010. The briefing paper spoke about how a social pedagogic approach would 'require rethinking the organisation of the working week to include more time for discussion, across teams, of young people's contexts and conditions' (p. 8).

The briefing paper went on to note that the approach of the social pedagogues to their practice had been broadly welcomed. The managers of the projects suggested that the pedagogues 'had been very good at establishing relations for young people, and skilled at dealing with potential difficulties, such as being different because of where they come from, their accent or merely being male in an all female staffed group. They have developed practical and creative activities for the young people' (p. 9). The paper describes one pedagogue creating a garden sculpture as a visible representation of participation, creativity and team work. In another example they demonstrate the importance of relationship building if workers are to develop a holistic assessment of a young person's needs. This example relates to:

> . . . *a young man who was described, in passing, as 'autistic', and difficult to communicate with, by his social worker. The social pedagogue took the time to ask the child questions and find out his interests, in a gentle and persistent way until he began to talk with her. The staff were astonished, and questioned why the social pedagogue took this approach, when they would've made far less effort. She responded in terms of the interest that the young person stimulated for her. How his brain worked, the way he linked events together. Through this approach she established a relationship of trust with him and subsequently*

discovered ways she could help him understand the situation he was facing. This showed the deep potential of the social pedagogue's integration of theory and practice to produce a positive effect for the young person.

(p. 9)

In the final report of the TCRU Social Pedagogy pilot project published in April 2011, the authors note the importance of developing inter-professional approaches and a focus on developing the independence of the young person. The latter they attribute to a focus on the concept of 'upbringing'. The social pedagogues engaged in the project were critical about the lack of clarity about the purpose and role of residential care in the UK. The report notes that 'in Germany, there was what was seen as 'erziehungsauftrag' (social mandate regarding upbringing) or overall vision of what society hopes to achieve for young people in general which did not appear to be articulated for young people in England' (Cameron et al., 2011: 77). They link this to ideas of what it is to be human in society (menschenbild). They note that, 'according to the social pedagogues, the menschenbild forms the foundation of any social pedagogy and is shared within the professional culture' (p. 77).

Clearly for an approach such as social pedagogy to be successful there is a need for a considerable systemic and organisational change in the agencies which currently deliver not just children's residential services but also youth services, social work services, community projects and others. As the Regional Youth Work Unit for the Northeast and the University of Sunderland note in their report, 'training in social pedagogy could improve the recognition of youth workers within the profession' (2010: 62). These issues are discussed in more detail in Chapters 6 to 9.

Summary

This chapter has looked at two of the major influences on the development of social pedagogy in the UK: the increasing penetration of social pedagogy into UK Higher education, and the broader interest in social pedagogy as a way of improving the delivery of residential children's services and consequently the experience of children and young people using those services.

The chapter concluded by highlighting a number of key issues discussed in later chapters – the importance of creativity in all social pedagogic activities and the potential relevance of social pedagogy in other services including youth work and inter-professional activity.

Exercise 1

Identify a piece of work you have been involved in which could be seen to encompass the three basic elements suggested by Hallstedt and Högström (2005) to be at the core of a social pedpedagogic curriculum. They were:

- Equality in the worker/student/user relationship.
- An emphasis on goal directed work – achieving things together.
- The use of non-traditional approaches such as artistic and creative activities.

Part Two: Social Pedagogy Theory

Chapter 2: The Emergence of Social Pedagogy Theory

Eriksson and Markstrom (2003) suggest that social pedagogy emerged from three distinct traditions – the continental tradition, the American tradition and the pedagogical tradition. They characterise these traditions in the following way:

- **The continental tradition** based on ideas of continuous learning, promoting liberation rather than the restriction of the individual, and on 'independent and intentional participation' (p. 12) and the strengthening of social interaction.
- **The American tradition** based on empiricism and a focus on individualised casework and therapeutic approaches. They quote Hessle who describes social pedagogy as the 'collective term for the advanced work for change that goes on with psychologically vulnerable groups, individuals, children, youth, adults and families in our society (Hessle, 1985:177, cited in Eriksson and Markstrom, 2003: 15). They suggest that such an approach has as its goal re-socialisation and integration.
- **The pedagogical tradition** influenced by Hegel's dialectical method through which individuals are constantly developing and which they suggest demonstrates social pedagogy's mobilizing perspective and people's capacity to change their situation. This perspective draws heavily on the work of John Dewey and Paulo Freire (see Chapter 3).

This book seeks to integrate these traditions and by doing so to demonstrate how social pedagogy can link the individual experience to a collective response so that it enables and empowers the people experiencing a range of social divisions to change their situations for the better.

Lorenz (1994, 2008) has suggested that social pedagogy came into use in Germany at around the middle of the 19th Century. He suggests that Karl Mager first used the term to refer to the societal aspects of education. Lorenz notes that 'social pedagogy signifies a concept which pays attention to the formation of society as a whole' (p. 92). He points out that Diesterweg, a Prussian pedagogue (see Chapter 3) noted that schools at that time were in thrall to the church and sought to create them as entities independent of the church and state. He further noted how Natorp (1854–1920) sought to develop a social pedagogy which prioritised the communal will over that of the individual. He argues that:

> *. . . this approach gives society, as the embodiment of what is rational, priority over the needs and interests of individuals, and social pedagogy becomes a programme for bringing about better social adjustment.*
>
> Lorenz, 1994: 93

Lorenz warns that this emphasis on social adjustment can actually have negative effects. He points to the way that social pedagogy became an instrument of the Nazi state in the 1930s. A primary reason for this was the introduction of the notion of 'Volk Community' (Volksgemeinschaft) which emphasised family, community, altruism and voluntarism. The underlying emphasis on social integration and community commitment were reflective of National Socialism's emphasis on creating identity through a strong state (Smith, 2008: 4). However, although any social theory emphasising the family and community can be used by various elements of the political spectrum social pedagogy has since been more positively represented. As Cannan, Berry and Lyons (1992: 73–74) have noted social pedagogy can be represented as:

> *. . . a perspective, including social action, which aims to promote human welfare through child-rearing and education practices; and to prevent or ease social problems by providing people with the means to manage their own lives, and make changes in their circumstances.*
>
> Smith, 2008: 5

The Thomas Coram Research Unit was commissioned by the Department of Health and the Department of Children, School and Families (now the Department of Education) to look at the efficacy of social pedagogy as a form of intervention in children's residential services (Cameron et al., 2011). This follows a gradual, but increasing, understanding of the importance of listening to different approaches to the provision of social professional work and in particular learning from our European neighbours (Lorenz, 1994; Hatton, 2001a, 2008; Lyons, Manion and Carlson, 2006).

Reporting on the initial stages of the Thomas Coram research, Petrie (2002) argued that:

> *. . . the pedagogue, exercising an emancipatory pedagogy and respecting children as social agents, could ensure that children and young people were themselves brought more fully into the discussion.*

Higham (2001) suggested that social pedagogy has a role in working with young people through the provision of personal advisor services. She suggested that this could overcome some of the deficiencies of current UK social work and that it could help to reclaim a broader concept of social work from the narrow managerial one which was becoming established at the time she was writing. She argued that 'the challenge for British social work is to establish broader European definitions of roles and scope of practice' (Higham, 2001: 28). As part of the TCRU research Cameron (2004) compared Danish and German practice in young people's residential care. She describes a German pedagogic student's statement that pedagogy is about 'heart, brains and hands' (we will look at this in detail in later chapters). She concludes that 'residential care in countries working within a social pedagogic framework see the discipline as a way of theorising the 'everyday' of living together that can be applied across many types of settings' (p. 149).

Further support for the possibility of introducing social pedagogy into the UK was provided through the report for the Department of Education and Skills by CPEA in 2007. The authors of the report Paget, Eagle and Citarella suggested that 'the principles of social pedagogy have much to offer in helping to develop a more holistic approach to work with young people' (CPEA, 2007: 3). This was consistent with the report of TCRU in 2006.

To evaluate the efficacy of social pedagogy to residential children's services in the UK TCRU were commissioned to run a pilot programme in 2008. Cameron et al. (2011: 2) describe the intention of the pilot programme as being to:

> . . . encourage a discourse within each children's home (in the pilot project) about the differences, and similarities, between the English and continental approaches and to promote learning about social pedagogy by working with it every day, generating curiosity among managers and staff who had been chosen specifically for their willingness to engage in mutual learning.

The children's homes chosen were located in the Northwest and the South of England. The project required the recruitment of social pedagogues in Europe and their placement in the children's homes. The interim report suggests that the project posed some challenges for social pedagogues relocating from Europe but that:

> The social pedagogues working in homes where there has been a continuous home and external manager, who have provided ongoing support for both the social pedagogues and the project introducing social pedagogy, seem to be most confident that they can demonstrate their different or fresh perspectives on practice.

> (p. 11)

The author will look in more detail at the potential of social pedagogy to improve outcomes for children and young people in public care in Chapter 6.

The concept of social pedagogy

How then can we conceptualise social pedagogy? Lorenz (1994: 92) argues that social pedagogy 'signifies a concept which pays attention to the formation of society as a whole'. He questions the direction in which social pedagogy may go but suggests that one alternative is for it to take on 'the critical conscience of pedagogy, the thorn in the flesh of the official agenda, an emancipatory programme for self directed learning processes inside and outside the education system geared towards the transformation of society' (p. 93).

Elsewhere he argues that the dialectics of care and control remain central to social pedagogic activity. He says that in 'all social interventions boundaries have to be negotiated rather than assumed and these boundaries . . . have to be legitimated not with the power we bring to bear in defining them for others but by elaborating a shared meaning of boundaries with all the participants' (Lorenz, 2002: 13). This is an issue that the author will return to in Chapter 4 when he looks at issues of pedagogy and power.

Kornbeck (2002) examined the potential relevance of social pedagogy to the UK context. He pointed out that in Europe social pedagogy is more then just about working with children and it is just as much about working with adults. Kornbeck concluded that the possibility of exporting social pedagogy to the UK was limited because of the different national educational traditions and the paradigms that undermine them. He questioned whether the UK social work tradition in education is ready to incorporate something so different and suggests that the litmus test will be whether or not social pedagogues are accepted as having equal status to social workers within the UK. As we noted earlier this was an underestimation of the degree of penetration of social pedagogy into UK Higher Education.

More recently he has commented on the absence of a social pedagogy tradition but suggested that there was now a sign of policy developments pointing to the 'emergence of a social pedagogy paradigm both in academia and in terms of careers' (Kornbeck and Rosendal Jensen, 2009: 2). This book is an example of the interest in the UK of creating such a paradigm, but at a broader level than the current preoccupation with residential and foster care (Cameron and Petrie, 2011).

In Scotland the Scottish Executive commended social pedagogy as sharing 'with the main tradition of social work the emphasis on human relationships and a holistic approach to social problems' (Scottish Executive, 2005: 3). At its core is a belief in the need for equality between professionals and people who use services and a commitment to placing relationships at the heart of social work. Jordan has reminded us of how central to good social work practice a focus on relationships has always been, particularly those relationships of 'empathy, equality and justice' (Jordan, 2007: 45).

Another example is provided by a recent Social Pedagogy Development Network (SPDN) meeting in the UK which sought to demonstrate the advances that social pedagogy has made in debates about social professional work within the UK. At the meeting a number of underpinning principles were outlined which included a commitment of attitude, mind set and ethos translated from the German *Haltung*. This was seen as expressing 'an emotional connectedness to other people and a profound respect for their human dignity'. *Haltung* was seen as encompassing:

- It's a 'stick of rock'
- Acceptance
- Playfulness
- Love
- Being allowed to love the child
- Empathy
- Stepping into others' shoes
- Curiosity
- All human beings have an equal value
- Equality – all on same level
- Humanistic democratic values
- Child as expert on their life
- The 'rich child' (risk)
- Respecting and working with a person's history
- Person/child centeredness
- Holistic view on human beings
- 'Underpins our own culture' – fits in with us

Some of the language here may need explication. The idea of the 'stick of rock' implies that the pedagogic relationship runs through all the work the pedagogue undertakes. The 'rich child' refers to the ideas of writers like Pestalozzi, Vygotsky and Diesterweg who talk about a child's potential and their opportunities for self-development (see Chapter 3). The use of the word 'love' may also present challenges to UK practitioners but should be seen as an example of Rogers' use of 'unconditional positive regard' in the counselling relationship.

Eichsteller and Holtoff (2011) demonstrate how *Haltung* connects to the concept of *Lebensweltorientierung* which they translate as life-world orientation and which is drawn from the social constructionist tradition (see below). They argue that the idea of life-world 'demonstrates social pedagogy's commitment to social justice by aiming to improve living conditions and social circumstances' (p. 37). In turn, 'social pedagogic *Haltung* does not refer to an attitude to individuals but provides the context for social pedagogy's aims and purposes at the level of community and society' (p. 38). As we will see in subsequent chapters, this conception of social pedagogy as operating at the structural level as well as in the interactions between individuals and families is an important element of the social pedagogic tradition which could emerge in the UK (Cousee et al., 2009).

The SPDN suggests that, in addition, social pedagogy is about enhancing happiness and well being, engaging in reflective practice, focusing on building authentic, strong and respectful relationships and sharing life space (this links to the concept of the

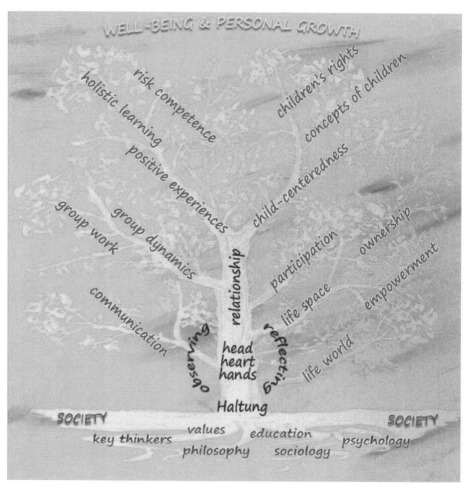

Figure 2.1   Social Pedagogy Development Network (reproduced with permission)

'common third' discussed below). In addition the SPDN suggests that social pedagogy aims to support social inclusion and tackle inequalities as a means to empowering the people pedagogues work with. They note the importance of head, heart and hands and suggest that a strengths-based approach which emphasises positive life experience is central to the pedagogic approach (Figure 2.1).

ThemPra (2008) suggests that the pedagogic role can be split into three key elements:

• The *private* – in which the pedagogue decides what they share about themselves with the people they work with.

- The *personal* – through processes of reflection the pedagogue establishes what to share with the person they are working with.
- The *professional* – the pedagogue uses theory, understanding, knowledge and skills to understand the reactions appropriate or inappropriate to the person with whom they work

Central to a pedagogue's activity is the use of head, heart and hands. The former enables the pedagogue to develop an understanding of the reasons for their intervention, the heart indicates the regard for and empathy with the person or group with whom the pedagogue is intervening, and the hands indicate the range of practical and creativity which the pedagogue uses in any intervention (Boddy, 2011).

Exercise 1

Identify aspects of your current practice which could be seen to encompass elements of social pedagogy – as outlined above.

Practice Focus 1

Social Pedagogy Development Network
'Never doubt that a small group of thoughtful, committed citizens can change the world. In fact, it is the only thing that ever has.' Margaret Mead

Our vision of the Social Pedagogy Development Network – a social pedagogic way of developing social pedagogy.
The Social Pedagogy Development Network has been set up as a grassroots movement for people and organisations that are interested in social pedagogy and want to nurture it at a local and national level. It is underpinned by social pedagogic principles about engaging in open dialogue, of valuing people and their experiences, of connecting with others in a democratic way. Social pedagogy is thus brought to life in people's unique ways, and through the exchange and relationships with others we can ensure that it grows on ideas and traditions from within the UK inspired by ideas and traditions from other countries. For this reason, the SPDN offers an 'oasis' that encourages a rich and colourful diversity of social pedagogy 'flowers' to blossom together. This means we provide the conditions for all participants to engage with each other and the themes or issues that you feel most passionate about, thus giving you the ownership of the SPDN.

> The SPDN is based on the idea of parallel action, that change occurs where people can pursue what matters to them by forming self-organised 'clusters'. Each cluster can initiate multiple, creative, and parallel action streams that reinforce each other, thus leading to change. Following Margaret Mead's words, we therefore aim to bring together small groups of thoughtful, committed citizens.

Embracing European models

We will examine in Chapters 4 and 10 the efficacy of the inclusion and community agendas to produce a reframed social pedagogy. It is worthwhile noting however that while they offer potential for moving social work forward they can also be reframed to promote a neo-liberal agenda (Ferguson and Woodward, 2009).

What about the other main challenge to our current practices, the relevance of European models to current practice? Hatton (2006, 2008) suggests that social pedagogy can remind us of the need to focus on relationship work and be less managerial in our practice. He argues that we can learn from pedagogic traditions in that they:

> . . . *may allow us to see the similarities as well as the differences between us, to recognize that truth does not reside in one set of culturally specific values but that ways of understanding, methods of working and commitments to social justice are often shared.*

Hatton, 2001a: 276

Fook (2002: 82) describes this as a process of 'transferability', or 'the ability of . . . theory to transfer meanings between different contexts'. We can learn from social pedagogic theorists and use that understanding to develop new theories and practices in the UK – a UK social pedagogy rather than the simple importation of existing social pedagogic theory and practice into situations which may not be receptive to knowledge paradigms which emerge from outside the UK.

There is evidence that such an eclectic approach is gaining favour in the UK (Cameron, 2004; Cameron, 2006; Cameron, McQuail and Petrie, 2007; CPEA, 2007). Petrie et al. (2006) have suggested that:

> *Social pedagogy is sometimes used to mean pedagogy conducted on behalf of society, rather than the more private pedagogy performed by parents. But the term can also denote work with more vulnerable groups in society. Different countries have different emphases and use slightly different terms.*

Petrie et al. (2006) quote a Dutch academic who argued that 'pedagogic theory is specially about relationships, child rearing relationships' (Dutch academic, interviewed as part of TCRU's Social Pedagogy Study).

Until the corpus of work emerging from the Thomas Coram Research Unit, social pedagogy had not been widely explored within debates around the work of the social professions within the UK, although it is a common approach within European social work traditions (exceptions are those outlined earlier – the BA European Social Work at Portsmouth, BA Curative Education at Aberdeen, the BA Social Pedagogy and Social Care at Liverpool Hope and the work of NCERCC). However, the Department of Health and The Department of Children, Schools and Families also expressed an interest in social pedagogy with the latter funding the pilot programme discussed above.

Hämäläinen, an experienced theorist of social pedagogy, argues that social pedagogy:

> . . . concentrates on questions of the integration of the individual in society, both in theory and in practice. It aims to alleviate social exclusion. It deals with the processes of human growth that tie people to the systems, institutions and communities that are important to their well-being and life management. The idea of social pedagogy is to promote people's social functioning, inclusion, participation, social identity and social competence as members of society.
>
> Hämäläinen, 2003: 76

Social pedagogy has a varied theoretical and practical tradition. An example is the Danish tradition of social pedagogy which draws on a range of sources from Freire to Kierkegaard (Hatton, 2001a). Central to this approach is the 'common third' which Aabro describes as a descriptive project or ambition within the pedagogical tradition of 'relations in social work in which there is a 'deliberate focus on the object as something outside the subject. The object being a 'common thing' which both parts in the relation can connect with' (see Hatton, 2006, 2008). Aabro describes the work of Husen who sees the key element of social pedagogy as being:

> . . . to be sharing something, to have something in common, [which] implies in principle to be equal, to be two (or more) individuals on equal terms, with equal rights and dignity (subject – subject relation). In a community you don't use or exploit the other (subject – object relation).
>
> Husen, 1996: 231, translated by Aabro, 2004

At the core of this relationship are notions of equality and respect and the eradication of unequal power relations. Cacinovic Vogrincic (2005: 336) makes a similar point when he talks about how the social pedagogue or social worker needs to develop a new language and concepts but makes 'the co-creation of solutions together with the client possible'. He suggests that such an approach is based on an agreement to work, common understandings, a focus on participation, a focus on strengths rather than weaknesses and finally what he calls co-presence, which he says is about, 'confrontations, understanding, agreements . . . (as) . . . sources of new experience and possible changes' (p. 338). He suggests that the key to these elements is the transfer of professional knowledge into professional action.

As Aabro suggests it is 'through a common or joint activity (that) the users and the social workers enter a subject – subject relation . . . (in which) . . . the professional is meant to 'forget himself' and the things around him – and devote entirely to the process and activity . . . the pedagogical challenge is to be able to realise activities which don't reflect the interests and needs of only one part, but instead seek to establish a *common* and *productive* activity.' (Aabro's emphasis in Hatton, 2006). One respondent to the review of social pedagogy in Essex undertaken by Eichsteller and Holthoff (2012) commented positively on their experience of using the 'common third', saying:

> *I now give great emphasis to using the 'Common Third' approach to building relationships with the young people. Seeking out opportunities via a seemingly endless scope of activities will allow for valuable bonding between two individuals or groups . . . I decided to utilise my time and get out of my comfort zone . . . I made the most of building positive relationships with all the young people. I remarketed myself as accessible and traded admin for activities with a sense of urgency.*

Petrie (2011) suggests that social pedagogues spend as much as 25 per cent of their training engaged in creative activities. Cameron and Moss (2011) argue that the Danish use of social pedagogy is based on a triple commitment. They quote Jensen and Hansen (2001: 5) who argue that:

> *Improving learning and developing options on behalf of ideals of individuals and society . . . pedagogical theories combine i) ideals of a good life (philosophy), ii) understanding of individuals and groups and their resources and needs (psychology and biology) and iii) understandings of social resources, values and demands (cultural and social sciences).*
>
> taken from Cameron and Moss, 2011: 10

Eichsteller and Holthoff (2012: 45) characterise the social pedagogic approach used in the Essex pilot as 'the art of being'. As they said, 'By using their own head, heart and hands to fully engage with children and build strong relationships they demonstrated that they genuinely cared about the children'.

An example of how to use the 'common third' from a student pedagogue

Borghill, a student on the BA (Hons) European Social Work at the University of Portsmouth in 2004, in analysing the usefulness of social pedagogy in a project utilising a social pedagogic approach with marginalised young people said:

The method involves pedagogues and service users concentrating on an activity together e.g. sports, repairing a car, or making a film, virtually anything. The point is that both the pedagogue and the service users have to be genuinely interested in the activity. This way their relation is moved to the background and does not seem important anymore. They are working towards a common goal, which is meaningful to all participants.

The activity has to be seen as a whole process where the service users are involved as equals in all phases, which are: choosing the activity, planning how to carry it out, actually doing it and in the end appreciating the result and evaluating the process. The young people must be given responsibility and the possibility to use their potential. According to Husen this should strengthen the young person's self confidence and identity and at the same time working together with other people requires social and communicative abilities such as understanding, cooperation and respect for the opinions of others and these skills will be developed.

Borghill, 2004: 16, quoted in Hatton, 2006: 116

Exercise 2

Consider practical ways in which each of Petrie's key principles of pedagogic practice could be applied to the following three scenarios:

	Child A (resident in a local authority children's home) and Adult A – residential care worker	Child B (a foster child) and Adult B – foster carer	Child C (has recently been issued with an ASBO) and Adult C – child's key worker from Preventing Youth Offending team
A focus on the child as a whole person, and support for the child's overall development.			
The practitioner seeing herself/himself as a person, in relationship with the child or young person.			
While they are together, children and staff are seen as inhabiting the same life space, not as existing in separate, hierarchical domains.			
As professionals, pedagogues are encouraged to constantly reflect on their practice and to apply both theoretical understandings and self-knowledge to their work and the sometimes challenging demands with which they are confronted.			

Pedagogues are also practical; their training prepares them to share in many aspects of children's daily lives, such as preparing meals and snacks, or making music and building kites.

When working in group settings, children's associative life is seen as an important resource: workers should foster and make use of the group.

Pedagogy builds on an understanding of children's rights that is not limited to procedural matters or legislated requirements; an emphasis on team work and on valuing the contributions of others in the task of 'bringing up' children: other professionals, members of the local community and, especially, parents.

Summary

This chapter began by outlining a conception of social pedagogy which draws on international traditions including the continental, American and social mobilisation views of social pedagogy. The concept of social pedagogy suggested draws on German notions of *Haltung*, the meaning of the pedagogic role and the way in which social pedagogues utilise 'head, heart and hands'. It closed with a brief discussion of the 'common third', a theme returned to in the following chapters.

Chapter 3: Key Thinkers

A diverse range of writers has been suggested as providing the theoretical core of social pedagogy. As noted above, Smith and Lorenz have argued that the development of social pedagogy can be traced through Mager, Diesterweg and Natorp. Hatton (2001a) has suggested that Danish social pedagogy can be seen as underpinned by the work of Kierkegaard, Grundtvig and Freire. Petrie has suggested that radical social pedagogy in the UK has its roots in Comenius, Pestalozzi and Frobel. She also suggests that UK developments are influenced by reformers such as Robert Owen, Thomas Barnardo, Emmeline Pethick and Mary Neal. Some of the most commonly cited of these thinkers are Pestalozzi, Vygotsky, Frobel, Dewey, Freire and the existentialist thinkers such as Kiergegaard, Grundvtig and Sartre. It is these authors whose work will be discussed in the remainder of this chapter.

Pestalozzi

Pestalozzi felt that for children to learn they needed to engage in activities. He argued that:

> I wish to wrest education from the outworn order of doddering old teaching hacks as well as from the new-fangled order of cheap, artificial teaching tricks, and entrust it to the eternal powers of nature itself, to the light which god has kindled and kept alive in the hearts of fathers and mothers, to the interests of parents to desire their children grow up in favour with god and in men.
>
> cited in Smith, 2008b: 1

Smith suggests that Pestalozzi's work is of relevance because of his concern with social justice, a belief in the potential to utilise everyday life experiences, the need for equilibrium between head, heart and hands. In addition, he demonstrates a concern with observation and reflection, he sought to combine education and work and to overcome what Smith has called 'the tyranny of method and "correctness"'. The Pestalozzian method is, according to Swile (2005: 162) 'based on a belief in the importance of sensory experience as it corresponds with the natural development stages'.

Vygotsky

Vygotsky was a Russian psychologist who developed ideas around children's development linked to the *zone of proximal development* which he defined as the range between what the child can do independently and what the child can do with appropriate assistance. As Swile (2005: 238) notes:

Learning involves the student working with other more capable peers or adults to solve challenging tasks. As the students develop abilities, less assistance is needed until eventually the task can be solved independently.

Cole and Wertsch (1996: 254) make a similar point when they suggest that in Vygotsky's method we can see the way that the 'less capable participants can participate in forms of interaction that are beyond their competence when acting alone'. As Vygotsky suggests:

The zone of proximal development defines those functions that have not yet matured but are in the process of maturation, functions that will mature tomorrow but are currently in an embryonic state. These functions should be termed the 'buds' or 'flowers' of development rather than the 'fruits' of development. The actual development level characterises mental development retrospectively, while the zone of proximal development characterises mental development prospectively . . . the zone of proximal development permits us to delineate the child's immediate future and his dynamic state.

Vygotsky, 1997: 33

Children achieve developmental progress, Vygotsky maintains, through processes of imitation. He argues that a key feature of learning is that it 'awakens a variety of internal developmental processes that are able to operate when the child is interacting with their environment and in cooperation with his peers' (p. 35). The internalization of these processes, Vygotsky argues, allows the child to develop independently.

This analysis of the way children, and adults, interact with each other and their external environment is a key insight which as we will see is central to the concepts of social pedagogy discussed in this book.

Diesterweg

Diesterweg, a German educationalist, was a contemporary of Kant, Froebel and Pestalozzi. In opposition to practice in 19th Century Germany he argued that it was important to emphasise the democratic nature of education, with a particular focus on the social context within which education took place. He argued that 'all (educational) theory separated from practice' is ineffectual and inappropriate (Gunther, 1993: 296) and regarded equality as the key to educational provision. He saw education as a means of improving people's situation and promoting self-development. Gunther (1993: 297) characterises Diesterweg's beliefs as follows:

Man is capable of development and improvement; activity as the reason for existence and a condition of the nature of man, faith in reason and a dialectical relation of thought and action; trust in the nature of man . . . taking pleasure in the world's variety; man's aspiration and ability to subject the world . . . to his own harmonious ends and organise them accordingly . . . harmony between the man and the community; development of all human powers to the benefit of the individual and society; fundamental equality of all men; and the unlimited diversity of human nature.

This clearly progressive, and almost post-modern, agenda can be seen to clearly influence the paradigms developed by social pedagogy with its emphasis on action, its notions of equality, within the context of the diversity of human experience and its promotion of aspiration. Perhaps the most significant element, in the light of the author's desire to link the focus within social pedagogy on relationships and individual approaches to a more systematic structural approach is the recognition of the importance of the dialectical relation between thought and action. This mirrors Marx's suggestion in the *Theses on Feuerbach* that while the task of philosophers is to describe the world, the point is to change it. ('The philosophers have only *interpreted* the world, in various ways; the point is to *change* it'. XI, Theses on Feuerbach, 1845 in Feuer, 1972: 286.)

Froebel

Froebel developed the idea of the Kindergarten system during the first half of the nineteenth century. He believed that human activity was essentially creative and productive. As such, he believed in developing educational environments which promoted creativity and were based on play and hands-on activities. His ideas later influenced Diesterweg.

Smith (2008a) argues that 'Froebel's continuing relevance has lain in his concern in learning through activity, his interest in social learning and his emphasis on the unification of life'. Swile (2005) has suggested that a key element of the work of Froebel was that the teachers should allow the children to learn by exploring freely and that the pedagogy they undertook should be child centred. Swile argues that for Froebel:

There is . . . no distinction made between the individual and the group. Children should be taught that they are part of a greater community and that the actions of any member of the community affect the community as a whole.

Swile, 2005: 170

Dewey

Dewey's work was heavily influenced by Hegel and particularly Hegel's use of dialectics. His views were progressive and sought to link individual and social development together. At its core, he believed that there were three central functions for schooling. First, there should be a symbiotic relationship between the school and home, school should prepare the child for an active life in the community. Second, it was important to focus on 'weeding' out those features of the school life which were inimical to a child's development. Third, it was necessary to provide a balanced and safe environment for the child.

Swile (2005: 185) argues that Dewey had a transcendental view of social reform in which the most important elements were:

> *The dignity of the child, the importance of experience in learning and disdain for traditional methods of education in which the child is viewed as a passive receptacle for the information the teacher imparts.*

Freire

A more recent influence on Danish pedagogy has been the work of Paulo Freire (Hatton, 2001; Eriksson and Markstrom, 2003). Freire (1972) argues that a key way in which people without power are marginalised is through a process in which their behaviour becomes pathologised and their human nature is constructed in a distorted way through what Freire describes as processes of indoctrination, manipulation and 'dominated consciousness'. He argues that as a result they lack the consciousness or understanding to decode their situations. He argues therefore for a process of deindividualisation, by which he means encouraging people to see the commonality of their situation. He suggests that this focus on the common interest can only be achieved through a process which he describes as *conscientanzo*. This is a process through which people not only become aware but act on that awareness.

Noting the influence of Freire, Eriksson and Markstrom (2003) suggest that the key contribution of Freire to social pedagogy is his emphasis on social mobilisation and emancipation. In this context they see social pedagogy as a means of initiating a process through which people mobilise their own resources. They quote the Danish writer on social pedagogy, Ronnby, who reflects on social pedagogy's potential to dynamise and mobilise groups. They argue that Ronnby's work suggests 'social pedagogy should stimulate people to change their situations and thereby also develop themselves during the process' (quoted in Eriksson and Markstrom, 2003: 18).

Other key influences

Some of these thoughts are reflected in existentialist accounts of the way people interact with society. Two Danish philosophers Grundtvig (1783–1872) and Kierkegaard (1813–1855) (Hatton, 2001; Hannay and Marino, 1998) have often been quoted by Danish professionals as a key to understanding Danish pedagogy. They helped form a critical view of established ideologies and power structures in society. Their thoughts were based on a humanistic and existentialist world view (a view of human nature = *menneskesyn*).

Grundtvig's thoughts and ideas sought to challenge what he perceived to be the oppressive dogma in theology politics and pedagogy. He was against all forms of indoctrination and believed that people have extensive unreleased resources which they could use to increase the quality of their lives. He aimed to mobilise these resources and obtain equality of opportunity for the education of all people regardless of their background. As Hatton (2001a: 271) notes, in Grundtvig's view:

> . . . *the underprivileged would only achieve liberation and freedom through education and enlightenment as this would enable them to become aware of the oppressive ideologies and power structures in society and to work towards changing them. He emphasised the importance of interaction, instead of unequal power positions, when helping people in their development. In this process both the helper and the helped would gain insight and growth. He criticised education and pedagogy for filling people's heads with facts and failing to give space for the qualities of the 'heart and the hand' to develop simultaneously.*

Kierkegaard's *menneskesyn* posited a holistic view of the human being, who should be understood as individuals but who were at the same time influenced by their environment. He suggested that to become self-aware people needed to reflect on their feelings, thoughts and actions. He questioned the balance of power between the rich and the poor and pointed out the need for dialogue, a focus on equality, respect for people's experience and a belief in their capacity to change the world around them. He however noted the uncertainties that can be caused by people suddenly having choices which they had not previously had. He suggested that the anxiety this could cause could lead to 'the dizziness of freedom' (Macquarrie, 1972; Gardiner, 1988). Gardiner (1988: 107) suggests that Kierkegaard sees the person as:

> . . . *an active subject who can envisage and respond to possibilities and where there is nothing that objectively compels me to opt for one response as opposed to another – here I am the sole arbiter and what I do is entirely up to me.*

Sartre is another existentialist (and Marxist) philosopher who has influenced the development of social pedagogy. For Sartre choice was at the heart of human existence. His central idea was that existence precedes essence. Contrary to the more deterministic forms of Marxism which were prevalent in the 1950s when Sartre was writing, he believed that all human beings have free will and are able to make a series of choices for which they must take responsibility. Blackham (1961: 132) summarises

Sartre's view as being that 'autonomous choice is not a mere wish or aspiration, it is not real unless it initiates action'.

Summary

This chapter has identified a number of important writers who have influenced the development of social pedagogy in continental Europe and remain an influence today. At the core of these writings are a number of key ideas about the relationship between the child or the human being and the world around them. They can be summarised as:

- A commitment to improve the lives of people through creating positive pedagogical environments.
- A belief that people's lives need to be seen in the whole.
- A belief that people learn best through reflecting on their actions.
- An emphasis on the use of physical activities to promote development.
- An emphasis on social justice and social change, particularly in the context of securing real improvements in people's lives.
- In all the above, an emphasis on the importance of creativity and imagination in promoting human development.
- A view that people are autonomous beings but they only become complete when they take action to change their circumstances. Understanding without action renders the person incomplete.

Case study 1

A tenants' group in a city in South Wales came together because of a common concern over the poor state of the properties they lived in. Members of the group had been consistently told that the disrepair was their responsibility and was due to their own inadequacy. A local law centre facilitated a meeting of the tenants who then realised that there were common problems in relation to the condition of all of their properties. This led them to question whether they were personally responsible or whether it was more to do with the quality of the social housing in which they lived. They took direct action against the local authority and secured significant improvements to all of their properties. Through this process of 'becoming aware' they became determined to use this experience to encourage tenants throughout South Wales to take similar action.

Chapter 4: Creativity, Inclusion and Social Pedagogy – The *CRISP* Model

Central to the concept of social pedagogy that the author believes needs to be introduced into the UK is the idea of creativity. Creativity is envisaged as an active process in which the social pedagogue/social professional works with the person using their service in a way which seeks to maximise their potential, increase their ability to make decisions and improve their life chances. The idea of creative activity is, as we will see, central to social pedagogy in Europe and to those educational initiatives based around social pedagogy which are occurring or have occurred in the UK. Petrie and Chambers (2009: 12) reviewing the importance of creative activity in the practice of Danish social pedagogues reported that creative work should be informed by democratic principles to the extent that pedagogues should 'respect children's social agency and their perspective on the world'. They suggest that the UK could learn from these approaches and that agencies such as the Children's Workforce Development Council and the Arts Council for England should promote creative activities in the work they support with young people.

An element of the work of Vygotsky which is less often commented on is his focus on creativity and imagination. He suggests that this must be linked to a focus on the future because 'if human activity were limited to reproduction of the old, then the human being would be a creature oriented only to the past and would only be able to understand the future to the extent it reproduced the past' (Vygotsky, 2004: 9–11). Our creative actions are in turn, he argues, based on our use of imagination which he argued is:

> . . . the basis of all creative activity . . . an important component of all aspects of cultural life, enabling artistic, scientific, and technical creation alike . . . whenever a person imagines, combines, alters and creates something new.

He suggests that central to the development of creative imagination is the need for the child (or adult) to have rich experiences, 'the richer a person's experience, the richer is the material his imagination has access to' (p. 15). He further suggests that there are within the development of creativity intellectual and emotional components and that they involve links between a person's internal and external worlds. As he says:

> Imagination is portrayed as an exclusively internal activity, one that does not depend on external conditions . . . The process of imagination per se, its direction,

at first glance, appears to be guided only from within, by the feelings and needs of the individual and thus to be wholly subjective and not based on objective factors. In actuality this is not true. Psychology long ago established a law according to which the drive to create is always inversely proportional to the simplicity of the environment.

Vygotsky, 2004: 30

Vygotsky sees this creative process as being dependent on both current environmental context and previous historical development. Creative developments then can be linked to processes of structural and class oppression. To free the creative imagination is to challenge the organisation of the society in which we live and to improve the life chances of the people we work with. Finally he reminds us of the 'agonies of creation'. As he says, 'creation is difficult, the drive to create does not always coincide with the capacity to create, and this is the origin of the agonizing feeling of suffering caused by the fact that the word does not capture the thought' (p. 39). Despite this he concludes by advocating the particular importance of cultivating creativity in school-age children (p. 87).

Fog (2003: 29) comments positively on Vgotsky's emphasis on the child's engagement in activities as the key to their cognitive development. She suggests, in the context of milieu therapy, that social pedagogic praxis is 'on the social and emotional side of raising a child into the socio political and socio cultural frame of a society'.

This is an approach which is consistent with a wide range of activities which have been taking place across the social sectors across Europe. In the spring 2009 edition of *Homeless in Europe*, the magazine of the European federation of national organisations working with the homeless (FEANTSA), there are a number of descriptions of the way in which arts and creativity can help with the empowerment of severely marginalised individuals and groups. The editorial of the journal claims that the examples quoted 'share the common achievement of having improved people's self-esteem, self-awareness and motivation, while challenging mainstream perceptions of homelessness' (FEANTSA, 2009: 3).

The magazine describes a number of initiatives across Europe. Matt Peacock, the chief executive of Street Wise Opera UK, welcomes the recognition of the importance of creative activity in tackling homelessness.

As Peacock notes:

. . . the confidence and self-esteem, increased communication and motivation that result from the arts have been shown to be the building blocks to help individuals move forward quicker and better.

FEANTSA, 2009: 4

In the same magazine, an interview with Hallvard Braein, a Norwegian film maker, describes how homeless people made a film of *Peer Gynt*. Orsolya Szele, a homeless journalist on Fedél Nélkül, who works on a street paper in Hungary, describes the Self Portrait Project, the purpose of which was to 'give a voice to those people who are not easily accepted to the majority of society' (FEANTSA, 2009: 8).

Hacking, Secker, Spandler, Kent and Schenton (2009) further describe the way in which an arts project in the UK sought to engage with people with mental health needs. They found small but significant increases in social inclusion and indications that people were building stronger immediate networks and significant improvement in the overall empowerment of participants. They suggest that there were five processes which could be seen to be linked to the increased empowerment of the participants. These were:

- Getting motivated – they describe this as the participants developing inspiration and pride in their art work which in turn gave them a sense of purpose.
- Expressing self – they argue that through creating art the participants began to discover and accept themselves. This was particularly true of those participants with complex mental health issues, difficult past experiences and those who self harmed.
- Connecting with abilities – one participant is recorded as saying, 'I can actually start to do things which I didn't think I could do before'.
- Rebuilding identities – this was evidenced by people expressing the view that they could achieve something through showing their art work to others, and in the process changing people's perceptions of themselves.
- Expanding horizons – they suggest that people began to see themselves as having an identity as an artist rather then as a mental health service user. They quote one participant who says, 'It's not just something that someone with mental health problems has produced, its something that an artist has produced and it just so happens that they have got mental health problems as well'.

FEANTSA, 2009: 12–13

Other articles from the magazine describe the work of DentroFuera – InsideOut, in Spain, the Verein Wohnen und Arbeit project, in Austria, 'Fashion with a Mission' project in the Netherlands and a number of UK projects all of which make similar claims for the efficacy of arts and creativity in working with marginalised and excluded people.

Chambers (2004) argues that creative arts can promote the health and well being of looked after children in that it 'encourages communication and helps children and carers to develop a language for talking about feelings' and that it results in 'personal empowerment, increased self-esteem and confidence, personal growth and social inclusion' (National Children's Bureau, Highlight, 212). The National Children's Bureau argue that engagement with arts and creative activities can:

- Enhance the self-esteem and resilience of looked after children and young people.
- Promote social inclusion.
- Improve sensory awareness.
- Help to counteract the consequences of childhood abuse and neglect.

National Children's Bureau, 2005: 2

They sought to promote such an approach across a range of sectors with a particular focus on ways in which such activities should be fundamental to the then developing Healthy Care Partnerships. They argue that:

> *Children and young people with disabilities, especially those who have limited means of communicating or interacting with others, often find creative arts a liberating and enriching experience.*

(p. 2)

This eventually led Chambers and Petrie (2009) to develop a *Learning Framework for Artist Pedagogues*, initially focusing on looked after children but based on principles which would be applicable in other settings.

Youth Music, a UK charity focusing on transforming the lives of marginalised and disadvantaged young people in the UK provides a further example of how creativity can produce positive outcomes. They see music as a means of enabling young people and allowing them to take control of their lives. Their work 'explores the outcomes that can be achieved through music-making projects for looked after children, and the barriers and facilitators to the effective delivery of these projects (Dillon, 2009: 4). They maintain that 'music-making can contribute to the development of a wide range of social and personal development outcomes for looked after children'. Among those identified were:

- Improved negotiation skills and co-operative working developed through group work.
- Learning to trust peers by relying on and supporting others in the course of the project.
- Developing both a capacity to express themselves and a stronger sense of self awareness through music-making, particularly by writing lyrics.
- Increased levels of self-discipline and a sense of responsibility for their actions.
- A sense of achievement attained through developing new music-making skills, the production of high quality musical outputs and performing.
- A positive sense of belonging and shared identity with other young people in care, which supported their understanding of the context in which they were living.

- Making friends through a positive activity.
- Developing positive relationships with adults (music leaders and carers) who modelled constructive ways of both working with others and dealing with conflict, and who live a life engaging in a positive activity such as music-making.
- Having the opportunity to have fun and 'escape' their problems through a positive activity.
- Cutting across all of the outcomes was increased confidence, both on a personal and skill-based level.
- Increased self-esteem and sense of self-efficacy.

Dillon, 2009: 4

Many of these outcomes match against those claims made for social pedagogy by the Social Pedagogy Development Network outlined earlier in the book. Indeed the link was made specific in a paper presented by a colleague of Dillon's at a research seminar at the University of Portsmouth in 2011 (Lonie, 2011). They are also consistent with the claims made for the efficacy of arts in mental health outlined by Hacking et al. above.

The National Youth Agency (2009) has also supported the use of creativity to promote the engagement of young people. Reviewing five projects across the UK they note how as the result of engagement with projects such as Rant (a fully equipped studio funded by Portsmouth City Council), Rolling Sound (a multi-media training provider in the commercial sector) and Gallery 37 Plus (a regional arts programme in Nottingham):

> *Some young people have been keen to move from engaging as participants with projects to undertaking roles as volunteers, or ultimately as workers/artists delivering activities.*

National Youth Agency, 2009: 3

Creativity and the arts can therefore provide us with an important way of remodelling the work of the social professions as an activity which can engage with both individual and social change. As Okitikpi and Aymer say in the introduction to their book on the art of social work practice, 'this book was born out of frustration and the desire to reconnect social work to its core principles, which we see as the building and sustaining of professional relationships with service users' (Okitikpi and Aymer, 2008: v).

Gray and Webb (2008: 184) warn however of the danger of sentimentalising the use of creativity, intuition and a focus on the aesthetic side of social work in that it can also be:

> *. . . indicative of a reactionary sentiment that partly relates to a sense of mourning, or a loss progressively engendered by the deskilling of the task, the degradation of work, the reduction of professional autonomy, the break-up of professional identities and the consumerist marketisation of clients as 'service users'.*

This mirrors some of the concerns regarding developing a focus on community as an alternative site of struggle for welfare practice (Hatton, 2008). Gray and Webb (2008: 184) argue instead for the idea of 'art as struggle' or of 'an art in the service of a politics of liberation' as being based on a sense of mutuality, partnership and equality. This aspiration for social work has been challenged by Healey (2008) who argues that instead of seeking a collective unity of purpose social work should continue to reflect the diversity of practice with which it currently engages. Lymbery (2009) and Charles and Wilson (2004) suggest a solution may be found by recognising but seeking to resolve the contradiction between competence and creativity in social work. Lymbery (2009: 114) suggests that in practices which involve assessment or evaluation skills the competence underpinning this work is insufficient and needs to be enhanced by 'the creativity that characterises best social work practice'.

This debate has relevance beyond social work. Lyons (2010) has shown how such an approach can have relevance across the helping professions. She demonstrates that play, music, drama, and awareness of the body can be employed in work with siblings, mental health users, people with physical and intellectual disabilities and in the care of older people. An understanding of the theory behind creative activity can promote, she argues, reflection and learning in a variety of contexts.

Pedagogy and inclusion

Inclusion is central to this development of a social pedagogy relevant to the range of professionals in the helping professions working in the UK. Social pedagogy should not just be seen as a technique but as a means of enhancing the lives of the people we work with. It is from this perspective that the *CRISP* model has been developed.

CRISP (Creation, Inclusion and Social Pedagogy) is an attempt to build a model of social pedagogy which makes explicit the need for creativity and inclusion to be part of the pedagogic/social work task.

It is now widely accepted that central to good social professional practice is a focus on inclusion (Hatton, 2008; Beresford and Hoban, 2005). Those involved with radical social and community work will appreciate the difficulty of achieving real inclusion rather than the often tokenistic attempts at inclusion which agencies seek to perpetuate (Arnstein, 1969; Hatton, 2008; Stepney and Popple, 2008; Ferguson and Woodward, 2009). However, one of the reasons for adopting such an approach is that it can produce a sense of localism which can connect us to the people with whom we work. Such an approach should be at the centre of any social professional activity.

Heikkila and Gulkunen (2003) have argued that social inclusion is a key principle which should be applied across all European countries. They suggest that a number of key principles should underpin this commitment to inclusion. These include:

- Involvement as a right and responsibility – there should be a democratic right for service users to be involved.
- Service user involvement should be central in the mission statements of all agencies.
- All service users should have access to services of sufficient quantity and quality.
- Research should be utilised to demonstrate the importance of service user inclusion.
- All services should have a culture of service user involvement.
- Users should be seen as recipients and actors – they should play a full role in decisions and debates around social care.
- Full accounts should be taken of users' networks as a way of maximising user involvement.

This is reflective of Foucault's view of why it is important to look at the local rather than structural aspect of political problems. He suggested that:

> . . . the problems which I try to address . . . which involve daily life, cannot be easily resolved. It takes many years, decades of work carried out at grass roots level with the people directly involved, and the right to speech and political imagination must be returned to them . . . the complexity of the problem will be able to appear in its connection with people's lives . . . the object is to proceed a little at a time, to introduce modifications that are capable of, if not finding a solution, then at least changing the givens of a problem.
>
> Foucault, 1981: 158–9

Although written in a different context this appears to be a clear articulation of a rationale for inclusion work. Service users have at last been recognized as having a significant role in the delivery, management and development of welfare services. This is reflected in the attention given to service user involvement in both the legislative and policy contexts and which cuts across all service boundaries and raises questions about service user representation (Hatton, 2008).

However it is important to recognise that the encouragement of involvement or inclusion is not the same as the way choice is presented in current prevailing social policy discourses. Jordan (2006) points to the potentially contradictory ways in which the question of choice is framed. He argues that an emphasis on choice and the user as consumer typifies the way the welfare state is developing, suggesting that 'the public infrastructure is redesigned so as to promote choice, giving citizen's information (for instance in the form of league tables) about the performance of hospitals, schools and care homes, so that they can switch to the best amenities' (Jordan, 2006: 142). Yet the reality is that within this scenario those without the material resources to make these choices real, lose out in a marketised form of welfare.

Inclusion and participation should therefore not be confused with a choice agenda which as currently expressed in the discourses of the Coalition government can be seen as a neo-liberal attempt to mask inequalities in existing provision and ensnare people into believing that they exercise control over the welfare services and welfare agencies with which they are involved.

Underpinning the need for a focus on inclusion is a commitment to recognise the agency of service users. Agency is characterised by Fook (1999: 200) 'as a sense of responsibility, of agency, an appreciation of how each player can act upon it to influence a situation'. Hatton, (2008: 94) has suggested that this would enable 'the creation of a radical practice based on notions of overcoming oppression, tackling discrimination/oppression and the creation of new cooperative social relationships, (which are) at the heart of any theory of social action'.

The importance of such an approach is evidenced by Akcelrud Durão (2006: 93) who argues that it is essential that for social action to be effective arguments for change need to emerge from excluded communities. This commitment to social action is recognised as a central tenet of social pedagogy by a number of writers including Hämäläinen (2003) (see also Chapter 10).

Hämäläinen (2003: 71) argues that social pedagogy has a distinct contribution to make to the conceptualisation of social work. He argues that social pedagogy starts from the premise that 'you can decisively influence social circumstances through education'. As mentioned in Chapter 2, he suggests social pedagogy's focus is on:

> *The integration of the individual in society . . . it aims to alleviate social exclusion . . . The basic idea of social pedagogy is to promote people's social functioning, inclusion, participation, social identity and social competence as members of society.*

> (p. 76)

Lorenz (2008) suggests similarly that social pedagogy can help us focus on the broader aspects of social intervention. Building on this, Marynowicz-Hetka (2007) suggests that social pedagogy can orientate practitioners towards the field of social action. She suggests that an important part of the social pedagogic approach is what she characterises as:

> *. . . reflection on the possibilities of learning . . . to act in/through and for communities . . . analysis of other solutions outside the traditional areas of social pedagogy, and their application to optimise and transform social practice.*
>
> (2009: 4)

This holistic view of social pedagogic interventions is reflected in some of the educational programmes offered at the University of Portsmouth. The diagram on the next page illustrates the way that social pedagogy and creativity are integrated into the social work curriculum at the University. Pete Shepherd (2012) a senior lecturer on the social work programme, says:

> *In the teaching of a creativity and empowerment unit the author and the students have worked alongside artists, poets and filmmakers who are engaged in changing perceptions and mainstreaming perspectives that have previously occupied the position of being 'outside' most institutions. The poster outlines and critically evaluates how such a curriculum has been developed with the involvement of service users and been delivered to student groups over the last two years. We use creative artefacts to assess students' knowledge and their ability to embrace the principles of participation in their consultative work with service users and carers.*

A recent *Participatory Arts and Social Practices* conference at the University of Portsmouth also developed these themes and illustrated the way in which artists and social professionals can collaborate to develop creative ways of working together (Hatton, 2011b).

The *CRISP* Model

We can now attempt to conceptualise the approach to social pedagogy which underpins this analysis and which the author argues distinguishes this account of social pedagogy from the traditions articulated by those piloting UK approaches to social pedagogy (Cameron et al., 2011). The approach being advocated suggests that the missing link between the creativity which it is suggested is essential to good, empowering practice and social pedagogy is the notion of inclusion. Creativity suggests a way of realising the potential of people working in and making use of welfare services. Social pedagogy as conceived in this book is predicated on equal partnerships between people working in and using welfare services. Both are central to the idea of inclusion. Inclusion provides the philosophical, practical and professional rationale for joining together creativity and social pedagogy and achieving a 'politics of liberation' as suggested by Gray and Webb (2008).

Service User involvement in Social Work Education at the University of Portsmouth

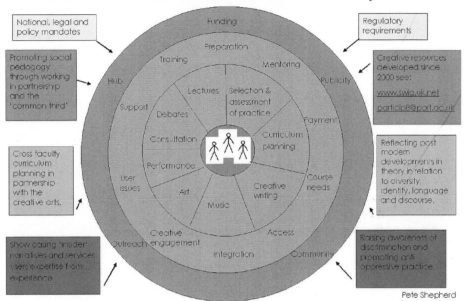

Figure 4.1   Service user involvement (Shepherd, 2012)

The key components of the *CRISP* model are:

Creativity – the utilisation of innovative approaches to deliver an experience to participants which is relevant to the dilemmas they face in practice and which repositions relationships at the heart of social care practice. This means designing and implementing a curriculum which challenges traditional didactic educational approaches by encouraging participants to develop work in partnership with those who use services and which adopts an approach which draws on drama, creative writing, performance, poetry, sculpture, music and other creative media.

Inclusion – the active involvement of the staff delivering and the people receiving (and their carers) day/residential locality and community based services in the design, delivery and implementation of new forms of practice. This principle is at the core of the social pedagogical methodology and will ensure that people receiving and using services are involved at all levels.

Social pedagogy – an approach to delivering services which is predicated on partnership between the social worker and user of services and which has as its base a commitment to relationship building, problem solving and social change.

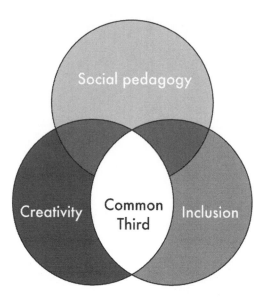

Figure 4.2   The *CRISP* Model

It stands in counter-position to more risk aversive approaches to service delivery and sees a considered approach to risk promotion as essential in the personal development of the individual.

This figure illustrates how taken together these concepts provide a way of conceptualising social pedagogy which allows us to see the importance of this approach. It links together creativity, inclusion and social pedagogy to suggest the importance of all elements to a reframing of our interventions, to provide an approach which is consistent with the humanistic principles underpinning the work of social workers, social pedagogues and social educators. Figure 4.2 illustrates the way in which these connections should be understood. The 'common third', with its focus on democratic practice, provides the core of this conceptualisation and the link between creativity, inclusion and social pedagogy. The Practice Focus opposite demonstrates the application of an approach which mirrors the use of the *CRISP* Model in practice.

Summary

This chapter has begun to develop a framework for social pedagogy which incorporates a variety of themes. Drawing on Vygotsky, the notion of *creativity* was developed as the first element of a conceptualistion of social pedagogy which illustrates the importance of using creativity with a wide number of people using welfare services including people who are homeless, who experience mental distress and with children and young people. It suggested that for such an approach to work it is important for such an approach to be *inclusive*. It concluded with an outline of the *CRISP* model, which it argued can take forward the debate around social pedagogy in the UK.

Exercise

Read the article re: film made by returning Irish exile migrants (*'A long way back'* – Jon McGregor, Guardian, Saturday 30th April 2011at www.guardian.co.uk/film/2011/apr/30/return-irish-exiles-film-jon-mcgreg or) and consider how this links with the concepts of social pedagogy, creativity and inclusion outlined above.

Practice Focus

ThemPra definition of creativity

Most definitions on creativity encompass four key characteristics of creativity, listed by the National Foundation for Educational Research (2006: 2) as:

1. **Using imagination** is the process of generating something original: providing an alternative to the expected, the conventional, or the routine. Creative insights can occur when existing ideas are combined or reinterpreted in unexpected ways or when they are applied in areas where they are not normally associated. Often this arises by making unusual connections, seeing analogies and relationships between ideas or objects that have not previously been related.

2. **Pursuing purpose** refers to the application of imagination to produce tangible outcomes from purposeful goals. To speak of somebody being creative is to suggest they are actively engaged in making or producing something in a deliberate way.

3. **Originality** can be achieved at different levels. Firstly, creativity can generate outcomes which show 'individual' originality – where a person's work is original in relation to their previous output. Secondly, outcomes may demonstrate 'relative' originality – where products are original compared to those of a peer group. Finally, creativity may result in work that is unique in relation to any previous work in a particular field, e.g. science or the arts, in which case 'historic' originality is achieved.

3. **Judging value** entails assessing the value of an outcome in relation to the task in hand – for example, is it effective, useful, enjoyable, satisfying, valid

or tenable? The criteria of value will vary according to the field of activity in question. In this way, creative thinking will involve some critical thinking in order to judge the value of a particular outcome.

Quoted in ThemPra Training Pack

Example – The Challenge Network

The Challenge Network brings young people together from diverse backgrounds and throws them in at the deep end. They take on physical, social and civic challenges that prepare them to design and deliver a project that will make a difference in their community. Along the way they learn key skills such as teamwork, leadership and communication, and are encouraged to develop trust in others, responsibility for themselves, understanding and empathy.

The Challenge Network is the charity that designs and delivers 'The Challenge', inspiring young people from diverse backgrounds to come together after writing their GCSEs and make their mark in the community. The Challenge Network is a registered charity established in April 2009, with offices in London, Birmingham and Bolton. The charity is funded by a variety of private philanthropists, trusts and foundations.

Our challenge: Our young people are struggling to come of age; they have lower levels of confidence and trust, weaker relationships and a lower sense of belonging than their contemporaries in almost all other developed countries.* The consequences on UK society can be seen in impacts on the economy, community participation, health and crime levels. There are few scalable programmes that tackle these issues by attracting and serving a broad group of young people.

Our aims: To help 15–16 year olds understand the responsibilities of adulthood, bring them together with people of different social backgrounds and motivate them to get involved in their local communities, thereby strengthening them.

Our approach: The way we achieve our aims is by providing intense, challenging experiences, reflection and high quality, consistent mentoring relationships.

Results to date: In 2009–10 c.670 young people from London and Birmingham took up The Challenge, with c.95% completion of the summer programme and all teams completing their community project. The social, ethnic and gender mix was broadly representative of the local population, with c.25% of participants eligible for free school meals and c.12% from independent schools. Our evaluation suggests 88% of young people who took up The Challenge agree that 'I am more likely to get involved in my community' and 85% agree that 'I feel more responsible for making a difference in my local community'. Over 80% of young people who completed The Challenge signed up to volunteer with another local charity for a further 6 months at our 'Milk Round' events on the final day of the programme.

2011 plans: Deliver programmes for 3,240 young people from London, the Midlands and the North West, establishing three regional hubs. Our key focus is on enhancing programme quality (more challenge, more service opportunities, even more varied social mix) whilst learning how to scale and preparing to franchise. Our plan is to scale to provide programme places for tens of thousands of young people per year by 2015.

Partners: The Challenge Network partners with a wide variety of organizations to deliver our programmes including Envision, Outward Bound Trust, the BBC, The Scouts and London Youth.

European Social Survey, NEF, 2007; *An overview of child well-being in rich countries*, UNICEF, 2007; *The Good Childhood Inquiry*, The Children's Society, 2009.

Chapter 5: Pedagogy and Power

There remains a missing element in this analysis. The model assumes equality between those engaging in social pedagogic interventions but does not explain how this occurs because, as formulated above, it lacks an analysis of the power relationships which underpin the practice relationship. Thompson (2007) has demonstrated the complex ways in which power can be understood – as psychological or personal, discursive or cultural and structural. He draws attention to the way it can operate as:

- Power to – a person's ability to maximise their potential and achieve their goals.
- Power over – similar to Lukes' first dimension of power in which a person or group has relations of dominance over another.
- Power with – a recognition of what people can achieve by working together.
- Power from within – which recognises the individual personal resources which people can bring to any situation.

Adapted from Thompson, 2007: 17

Within European social pedagogy discussions of power are often influenced by a social constructionist analysis of power relations. Within the social constructionist paradigm, there is an emphasis on the inter-relationship of the individual and society which derives from the work of Berger and Luckmann (1971: 210–11) who saw 'human reality as socially constructed reality'.

Clarke and Cochrane (1998) suggested that social construction 'implies an active process of definition and redefinition in which some issues are widely understood to be social problems, while others are not' (1998: 9). At the centre of this process is what is regarded as a *common sense* understanding of what constitutes a 'social problem'. Underpinning this understanding is a complex process through which people with power marginalise and exclude those without power so that the responsibility for their isolation and marginalisation becomes attributed to their lack of capacity to secure their own interests and needs. It is through such a process that we see, particularly at times of economic or political crisis, welfare recipients (currently disabled welfare recipients), single mothers, and unemployed young people constructed as social problems and held responsible for the problems facing the public sector in particular.

However the key to the social constructionist position is to see people as not merely acted upon but as actors in their own right (Burr, 1992). How then do people engage with processes of social change? It is important to recognise the diversity of the human condition: people are social actors but their capacity for action is determined, to some extent at least, by the social, political and economic environments in which they find themselves. Their capacity to 'act' can be impacted upon their psychological and social experiences. This is not to discount the existentialist focus on free will and the debates around agency discussed above. However it locates these ideas in a context where they are impacted upon by broader structural factors.

Hinshelwood (1978) suggests that we should take account of the ways in which communities can fragment the sense of personal identity which is an intrinsic part of people's capacity to act. He pointed to the ways in which communities which are under threat, and in which there appears to be no prospect of improvement, often search for 'an omnipotent helper' who 'never exists' and therefore 'dramatisations feed us a vicious circle which leads to a self-defeating state of demoralisation – a demoralisation trap' (Hinshelwood, 1978: 140–1). He further suggests that 'the affective networks of institutions have come to be remarkably efficient at exploiting individuals' feelings, states and experiences, reifying bits of human beings and estranging them from the human world' (Hinshelwood, 1982: 82).

These comments are also reflective of the writings of Frantz Fanon and Albert Memmi, two writers who were engaged in the struggles for independence from France in the 1950s. Fanon (1978) suggested that colonisation impinges on the individuality of the colonised person and people. He argues that their experiences become transformed because the colonisers seek to frustrate the colonised, 'binding him with prohibitions of all kinds' (Fanon, 1971: 175). The ruling elite's political and economic power, Fanon suggests, results in the colonised experiencing a feeling of inferiority (dependency complex) which he argues is a consequence of relations of domination and power. Remove the domination and the accompanying psychological and identity stereotypes dependent on it and the dependency complex will become attenuated, removed.

In a similar vein, Memmi argues that 'colonisation can only disfigure the coloniser' (Memmi, 1990: 213). Writing about the experiences of being a black/non Moslem person in French Tunisia in the 1950s, he describes the dialectical relationship of coloniser and colonised, pointing out how one cannot exist without the other, how colonisation weakens the colonised. Memmi suggests that to overcome this experience of colonisation the colonised, that is the person without effective power, needs to reclaim their own power and re-establish their own identity.

An understanding of how power and power relationships operate is central to the development of a critical social pedagogy. In this context, power needs to be seen as a multi-dimensional concept, in which power can be seen as a process in which people are acted upon but are also able to resist (Foucault, 1980). One key analysis of how power operates is presented by Lukes (1972). He suggested that power has three dimensions:

1. In cases of observable conflict A exercising power over the actions of B.
2. By preventing conflicts arising in the political arena through control of the agenda.
3. By preventing issues emerging through ensuring that people do not understand where their true interests lie (similar to Marx's concept of 'false consciousness').

Foucault points to the way in which the exercise of power becomes hidden when he says 'it became necessary for disciplinary constraints to be exercised through mechanisms of domination and yet at the same time for their effective exercise of power to be disguised' (Foucault, 1980: 106). This is similar to Lukes' third dimension of power discussed above. Foucault argues that it is necessary to analyse how power operates, 'on the basis of daily struggles at grass roots level, among those whose fight was located in the fine meshes of the web of power' (p. 116).

Foucault further suggests there is a role for what he calls *specific intellectuals*: 'magistrates and psychiatrists, doctors and *social workers*, laboratory technicians and sociologists have become able to participate, both within their own fields, and through mutual exchange and support in a global process of politicisation of intellectuals' (1980:127 – my emphasis). This is an important insight for social professional practice more generally. Social workers, social pedagogues and other professionals need to be aware of the way in which power relations operate to (a) confuse and mystify the way power operates (b) lead people to blame themselves for their inability to change their situation leaving them demoralised and unable to see their capacity to act and (c) fragment people's sense of social reality and their own social identity but also to provide opportunities for people to engage in social action to change their situation.

This idea of specific intellectuals has commonalities with Gramsci's concept of the 'organic intellectual'. Gramsci saw intellectual activity as not being something which is undertaken by a professional or political elite, but as an activity in which people explore their understanding of the world around them. He believed that people construct their own meanings and understandings of the world and that they are often in a better place to understand the world around them than people who profess to being able to articulate a world vision for them. In his conception organic intellectuals are those people who develop their understanding through engagement with social struggles.

This could be achieved, Gramsci suggested, through what Mayo has characterised as 'a transformative and emancipatory' adult education (Mayo, 1999: 127). McLaughlin (1995, 1998) writing about the experience of Irish Travellers makes a similar point when he talks about how the Travellers' movement in Ireland had moved from a situation where it was dependent on the support of engaged and committed intellectuals and practitioners to one in which it has its own 'ethnic intellegentsia'.

To begin this process of change involves recognising what Foucault has called 'the manifold forms of domination' in society (p. 96). To do this we need to develop, in Foucault's worlds, 'ascending analysis of power' starting from:

> . . . *its own infinitesimal mechanisms, in which each have their own history, their own trajectory, their own techniques and tactics, and then see how these mechanisms of power have been – and continue to be – invested, colonised, utilised, involuted, transformed, displaced, extended etc, by ever more general mechanisms and forms of global domination . . .*
>
> Foucault, 1980: 99

He argues for an analysis of power in which the way power is exercised is 'annexed' by the powerful and concealed so that it is not always easy to assess who is exercising power or to show how this happens in indirect as well as direct ways. To counter this he suggests we need to examine the exercise of power from the most basic to the most significant levels.

Importantly, Foucault points to the way in which power is localised and as a consequence he suggests people are able to engage in acts of resistance and rebellion to transform their situation. Foucault talks about the circulatory nature of power in which he says individuals are 'always in the position of simultaneously undergoing an exercise in this power. They are not only its inert or consenting target; they are also the elements of its articulation. In other words, individuals are the vehicles of power, not its point of application' (1980: 98).

This is a crucial insight as it allows us to see the many dimensions of power. He points to the way in which people can be actors and not just acted upon. This is consistent with some of the underpinning theoretical discussions in Chapters 2 and 3. There is a clear link here with the idea of a 'common third' which posits that there should be an equal relationship between the worker and the person using services. If we view this relationship as one in which the worker has the power but cedes a degree of power to the person they work with then we will reduce the efficacies of our intervention and be in danger of fragmenting the identity of the person we work with by refusing to fully acknowledge their capacity to act.

An interesting application of Foucault's work can be found in the writings of Chris Weedon (1979). Weedon applies Foucault's analysis to feminist discourses and it is illustrative to focus on her development of the concept of *reverse discourse*. Echoing Foucault, she points out that we should not engage in simple bipolar analyses of power and powerlessness. She suggests that different groupings operate in terms of their own 'force of field relations'. She describes these as 'relations of power which take specific form in particular societies, organised for example through relations of class, race, gender, religion and age' (Weedon, 1987: 110).

She further suggests that these processes can constitute a *reverse discourse* when she suggests that 'the degree to which marginal discourses can increase their social power is governed by the wider context of social interest and power within which the challenges to the dominant are made' (p. 111). Again this provides an important way of centring the experience of people who use services within social pedagogic discourse. The reverse discourses of which Weedon writes are an important means of challenging power relationships and are therefore central to the *CRISP* model discussed in Chapter 4. It is through processes of inclusion that people who are marginalised and excluded become central to social pedagogic activity.

By promoting this understanding of power as an activity which can be undertaken by the most marginalised and excluded, we can see how social pedagogy can contribute to the resolution of problems across a wide spectrum of welfare activity including adult social care, mental health, substance misuse, homelessness, and learning disabilities in addition to its contribution to children's services. This is not to deny that social professionals currently exercise an unequal power viz-a-viz people using services. However, we are talking here of a form of activity which has the potential to be more emancipatory in its practice than current social welfare practice. This conceptualisation of reverse discourse and the acknowledgement that it means centring currently excluded individuals and groups in our practice is therefore an important element of what we need to do.

An author whose work is seldom mentioned in discussions of social pedagogy is Che Guevara. We are familiar with his revolutionary activities which have been well documented in popular publications such as *The Motorcycle Dairies*. However central to his writings is an engagement with the need to explain, educate and emancipate. He used the concept of 'example' as an educational method and argued that 'both the good and the bad examples are very contagious and we must try to pass on the good examples working on people's conscience' (Turner, 2007: 49). He suggested that if an example does not accord with the life experience of individuals, if it is not real or tangible, it loses its ability to influence or bring about change. To overcome this, he suggests, examples need to be based on practical activities.

Turner suggests some key principles underpin Che's pedagogical activity including 'combining the rationality of the analysis with the emotional to work on the feelings; combining the objective with subjective dose of optimism about social development; linking every event with its social impact with the individual' (2007: 84). Che suggested that the pedagogic role consisted of a series of dialectical contrasts between 'theory and praxis, decision and discussion, leadership and guidance, analysis and synthesis' (p. 96).

These ideas are important because they are reflective of the concerns we raised in Chapter 4 when discussing the *CRISP* model and are also about how we can operationalise a concept of pedagogy which meets people's needs and which enables them to be part of an emancipatory process which can allow them to change their situation. How then can we actualise the pedagogic role in a way which recognises the power of the person with whom we work?

A writer who could contribute to a wider understanding of social pedagogy is Yuval-Davis (1997, 2011) who talks of the need to develop new forms of political engagement if we are recognise difference, yet build coalitions for change. She describes what she calls a process of *'transversal politics'*. Central to this is what she has called the processes of *'rooting'* and *'shifting'*.

By this she means that each participant in the dialogue, which is part of the process of securing change, brings with her the *rooting* in her own group and identity, but tries at the same time to *shift* in order to put herself in a situation of exchange with women who have different groupings and identities. The process of mutual understanding which emerges creates the potential for people to work together to change situations that they may find discriminatory or oppressive. In this sense transversal politics are not just coalitions of 'identity politics' groups which assume all members of such groups are equally positioned and culturally, socially and politically homogeneous. Gender, class, race, ethnicity and all other dimensions of specific positionings are taken into consideration as well as the particular value systems and political agendas of the participants in the exchange (Yuval-Davis, 1997a: 204).

A vital component of such an approach is that the process of rooting and shifting should not involve what Yuval-Davis calls *decentring* – losing one's own roots and set of values, and the process of shifting should not homogenise the 'other' – 'the transversal coming together should not be with members of the other group *en bloc*, but with those who, in their different rooting, share compatible values and goals to one's own (Yuval-Davis, 1997a: 206). She warns however of the need for realism: 'transversal politics are not always possible, as conflicting interests of people who are situated in specific positionings are *not* always reconcilable' (Yuval-Davis, 1997(b): 130).

However, despite this caveat, it is clear that the ideas outlined above and drawn from social theory, political theory and sociology can contribute to a deeper understanding of the potential for social pedagogy to engage with emancipatory discourses and promote social and not just individual change. In particular the positioning of people facing marginalistion and exclusion at the centre of our work and the valuing of their discourses can contribute to the development on new forms of practice.

Summary
Building on Chapter 4, this chapter has explored the importance of power to analyses of social pedagogy. Drawing on social constructionism it looked at how power

impacts on the individual and how the individuals can themselves exercise power. It argued that power is multi-dimensional and that we as social professionals can exercise power in an emancipatory way. It concluded that social professionals can, by understanding how power operates, subvert dominant discourses and construct new relationships.

Exercise

(i)   Consider how these ideas of the exercise of power and the notion of 'rooting and shifting' relate to the *CRISP* model (outlined in Chapter 4).

(ii) Identify an example from your own practice where it might be possible to draw upon the concept of pedagogy in meeting people's needs and enabling them to be part of an emancipatory process which could result in service users taking action to change their own situation.

(iii) Apply the notion of 'reverse discourse' to contemporary discourses around the Big Society.

Part Three: Social Pedagogy Practice

Chapter 6: Reflections From European Students Who Have Studied in the UK

One way of evaluating the possible impact of social pedagogy across welfare services in the UK is to listen to the accounts of social pedagogues who studied and undertook work placements as part of their experience on the BA (Hons) European Social Work and Social Care (BAESW) programme at the University of Portsmouth. While researching this book I contacted a number of ex-students and asked them to comment on their experience and reflect on their learning and on the efficacy of social pedagogy in a UK context.

This chapter looks at the experiences of these social pedagogues and at their perceptions of what social pedagogy is in addition to some of the practice situations in which they were able to demonstrate social pedagogic principles. They were asked what the most important theories used by social pedagogues were. Maria said:

> It is important for social pedagogues to know and understand how the society works. Perspectives of a welfare system . . . so theory about the society and the development of society is important . . . in Denmark, the government closes more and more special institutions because people with disabilities should be included in society as much as other people. So I think that as a social pedagogue you have to engage individual knowledge about the people you are working with.
>
> correspondence with Maria, August 2010

Another student, Sujato, describes using a more individual philosophy. She says:

> I . . . work with children from unfortunate backgrounds such as poverty, drug abuse, sexual abuse, violence and mental (health problems). We use attachment theory, theories of the self, creating and building trust, theories of child development. I also use the work of Kari Killen.
>
> omsorgssvigt er alles ansvar, 1993

Karina describes the contradictions of using theory in her practice. She says:

> I think it depends on the institution. Some work with Regio, Amelia, others, Marte, Meo. The most common overall strategy (philosophy), which overrules

any choice of method, and one that is visible or just in the public institutions but also within government and the private sector is empowerment (selvforvaltning). Based on liberal ideas/market mechanisms, which focuses on individualism and low cost . . . these two ideas contradict in practice, as it is difficult to address service users at an individual level at the same time as keeping the cost down. Quality costs money.

She goes on to talk about the eclectic nature of her practice:

To me the most important theories depend on the service user that I am working with, meaning that there is a huge difference in choice of theories, if I am working with different ages, sexes, ethnic minorities or (people with) mentally disability. I use theories from geography (I try to analyse landscapes for children/ playgrounds/schoolyards etc.) theories from anthropology in reflecting my own presence in the field I am studying. Theories from sociology have been useful when working with ethnic minorities . . . I guess my point is, that a good pedagogic adjusts the choice of theories to suit the purpose and should therefore be well read and keep up to date with recent theories in order to cope with changes in society . . . she/he should not be afraid to cross over the professional academic boundaries in the search for useful theory.

correspondence with Karina, August 2010 – my emphasis

In the correspondence the author asked the former students to define the 'common third'. Maria said:

The 'common third' is when the social pedagogues and the people they are working with (have) a working process towards some kind of common goal, which isn't dependant on their relation. So I'm not doing a certain activity with a 19 year old boy at a residential home because I need to (teach) him something during the activity, but because we need to help each other doing it. The 'common third' is reaching a common goal together by cooperating (my emphasis).

Karina suggests that the 'common third' should be understood as an activity. She said:

Instead of giving the service user time to focus on individual problems, identities or conflicts among the service users, pedagogues can arrange an activity which engage(s) the service users so (the) focus (is) removed for the above mention to the activity itself. The idea is that people will achieve a feeling of belonging to a community when they work together on a project and that that will pro- mote tolerance and a greater understanding of social behaviour. The service users will see and be able to present other sides of each other's personalities which allows the service user to 'be someone else', to show competencies that (have) not been seen earlier and to restart and add new elements to his/her social identity.

Sujato defines the 'common third' as an activity which she says is:

Performed by the pedagogue and child together. As the focus is shifted away from the persons participating and on to the project which is being created. The 'common third' is used to strengthen the relationship between child and pedagogue and observe the child's behaviour in this situation.

Irene focuses on the way the 'common third' can provide a way of developing relationships with service users:

The 'common third' is the thing or the situation where the professional pedagog can build a relation with the client through something else. The 'common third' is an icebreaker in the relationship between the two and (is) used in the social work to get access to the client. The client feels that they have something in common which makes the pegagog more human, more friendly, than just another professional pedagog/social worker. It could be an activity or an experience that they have together which feels unique in a positive way.

Kristina defined the 'common third' as:

putting the emphasis on the mutual activity between the service user and the pedagogue acknowledging that meaningful relationships support the development of identity and self-confidence and also increase the feeling of well-being . . . pedagogy has the focus on activities exercised within the frame of the direct work with the service user, or a group of service users, and the values and skills gained from these activities and relationships.

However she warns that:

This approach fails the battle of injustice and discrimination on a socio-political level due to the fact that most of the professional focus is limited to the encounter between the service user and the pedagogue.

They went on to describe elements of their practice (notes from correspondence with author):

Maria works with a 19 year old man. She says:

He has ASD and other mental disabilities. He communicates verbally but has lots of problems understanding other people when they communicate verbally. Also, he doesn't understand unwritten social rules . . . he likes being with other people and identifies himself with other people. But when he doesn't understand other people he gets frustrated. The only way he knows to react when he gets frustrated is to get violent towards other people and himself. He doesn't understand if I tell him to behave. That's a very abstract word for him. I have several times sat down with him one to one. We wrote down simple concrete words which define how to react in an appropriate way towards himself and other people . . . for this young man it is very helpful to have instructions to everything with simple words telling him what to do and how to do it . . . we help (the people we work with) to get tools and strategies to become part of Danish society.

Karina undertook voluntary work for an organisation dealing with young men aged 14–20 from an ethnic minority community in Vesterbro (Copenhagen). She says:

I was asked to engage the young men in political issues, as they time and again showed lack of basic knowledge regarding work, education, democracy, rights and duties etc. The organisation had no money to support the project . . . I contacted four of the biggest newspapers, who agreed to deliver papers everyday for three months for free. The purpose was to talk about the articles, to ask the young men to comment . . . and to show them the diversity of newspapers and how the same piece of news was presented differently. My hope was for them to start an interest in reading and reading news. To focus on the importance of diverse opinions where theirs was just as valid as anyone else's.

Sujato works at a residential home/children's centre for children aged 0–6 who due to neglect/abuse have been removed from their homes. She says:

The children live here and are observed ... in order for the social professionals to find the right foster family or further institution for them to spend the rest of their childhood. I am the main carer (what we call the primary pedagogue) for a five-year-old boy. It is my job to build a relationship with him and work on his trust and self-esteem. It is my responsibility to care for him, buy clothes and toys, make doctor's and dentist's appointments. It is also my job to cooperate with the boy's parents and as well as with the social worker and psychologist handling his case.

Irene describes her work with children aged 6–12. She says:

I work with children age 6–12 years old who are placed outside their home. They don't live at home because their parents can't look after them, and most of them are neglected and their behaviour is socially unacceptable. We work with environmental therapy (Lars Rasborg has written some books about it). Most of them spend the weekends with family and Monday to Friday they live and go to school where I work. The social work with these children is to teach them more socially acceptable strategies to cope with life.

Kristina also works with children in the same age range. She says:

I work in a Danish kindergarten with children in age range 2–6. I will not define myself as a social pedagogue, just as a pedagogue because I work in 'the normal' area. In Denmark we distinguish between 'the normal' area and 'the special' area and normally we say that social pedagogues work in 'the special' area.

... In my work we want to give the children a secure and loving fundament on which we can challenge and educate them so that they are ready for school and for life in Copenhagen/Denmark. Beside that we put a strong emphasis on social skills, such as engaging in a group, being a

> good friend, taking care of each other, negotiating, talking to each other
> about the difficult stuff, making up after a fight and so on. We also teach
> the children to listen to messages so that controlled activities can work . . .
>   . . . We focus on the individual in the group, where the parents focus
> on the individual only. We do that by trying to support all children so that
> they can engage in relationships with other children and in group activities.
> This means that we give more support to children in need of help in that
> area.

Examples of dissertation study undertaken by students on the BAESW programme

The range of studies undertaken by students on the BAESW is illustrated by the titles of the following dissertations undertaken by students on the programme. They reflect not just the efficacy of social pedagogy across areas of social professional practice but also the range of countries where social pedagogic approaches can be adopted. These and other dissertations convinced the author of the applicability of social pedagogy across a range of services within the UK.

Is there any difference in the way people with learning difficulties speak up for themselves in different countries? A comparison of experiences of the advocacy movement of people with learning difficulties in England and Spain (2008)

Empowerment: A comparative study between Denmark and the UK (2007)

Marginalised youth: A comparative study between Denmark and England (2007)

An evaluation of whether a combination of social work methods found in Denmark and the UK can provide the framework for a more sufficient and holistic approach within social work, capable of meeting the need identified in relation to marginalized young people.

The empowerment of young people at risk through sport and outdoor activities (2004)

Summary

This chapter explores the voice of those international students from social pedagogic backgrounds who have contributed to debates about social pedagogy, while studying on the BAESW at the University of Portsmouth. It showed how they developed their theoretical understanding of social pedagogy, how they conceptualised the 'common third' and how they have utilised their knowledge in practice since completing the programme.

> **Exercise**
> Think of an example from your own practice where an activity you participated in with a young person could be characterised as using the 'common third'. What features of the activity would bring it within this definition

Chapter 7: Social Pedagogy, Children's Services and Looked After Children

Much of the attention around social pedagogy in the UK has focused on the efficacy of social pedagogy within children's residential services. This is partly the outcome of perceived problems within UK children's services, including the Climbié enquiry and the Laming Report, developments around *Every Child Matters*, the Baby Peter case and the second Laming report in 2008. Taken with the Munro report in 2010 these suggested there was a need to reconsider the way children generally, and those in state run residential care specifically, were experiencing that care.

As noted in the introduction, the impetus for looking at new ways of delivering residential children's services also had external drivers. These included: the growing interest in international and European social work; the development of degree programmes utilising a social pedagogic approach; and a developing interest in social pedagogy as a particular approach to delivering services.

Almost all of this attention was directed around work with children, with a number of exceptions such as Hatton (2001a, 2006) and Higham (2001). The former was concerned more with looking at how social pedagogy could revive an increasingly managerial discourse within social work by focusing on the relationship-enhancing and empowering aspects of social pedagogy. The latter author suggested that there were links between the role of personal advisers within the Connexions service and that of pedagogues, and that social pedagogy could contribute to a revived agenda for services working with young people.

The concerns around children's residential services and more specifically the way the state intervened with children, young people and their families, were given added impetus by the death of Victoria Climbié, the subsequent Laming Report and the policy developments which emerged thereafter including *Every Child Matters* and, later, *Care Matters*. The potential role of social pedagogy as an important element in the development of children's services was identified in the 2005 Children's Workforce Strategy (Department for Education and Skills) and in a discussion paper for the same department also in 2007.

One of the earliest examples of the use of social pedagogy in residential care in the UK was that undertaken by the Camphill Rudolf Steiner School in Aberdeen. With the University of Aberdeen, Camphill developed a BA (Hons) in Curative Education. Writing about this development Jackson (2003: 1) has said that the degree 'facilitates the concurrent acquisition of theoretical insights, practical skills and personal growth'. He pointed to the way in which curative education was multi-disciplinary involving education, therapeutic and medical activities and social care. Central to the Camphill approach was the use of creative arts and crafts. At its core was an emphasis on human relationships.

In a later article, Jackson (2006: 65) suggested that the concept of curative education could provide the focus for a radical transformation of residential services. He suggested that 'in essence the curative educator is a social pedagogue who has chosen to work with children with special needs'. He argues that there are three key concepts underpinning the approach to curative education/social pedagogy undertaken in Camphill. These are:

Mutuality – in a similar way to the 'common third', he suggests that this means an equality of relationship and a focus on the quality of interactions. This means, he suggests, that 'the negotiation of power sharing across inequality makes a reality of the rhetoric of empowerment' (p. 70).

Rhythmicity – by this he means that the workers and the children establish a group cohesion which allows them to work in a rhythmic way together.

Spirituality – here the focus is on promoting dignity and valuing others, establishing a sense of cordiality relating positively to each other and being 'at ease with the world around them' (p. 71). Again there are links to the concept of *Haltung* outlined in Chapter 2.

From within a similar tradition, Smith (2007: 7) has suggested that social pedagogy is operable in a range of organisational settings but that 'a pedagogy for sociality has a ... different character, one that involves engagement with associational life, civic society and local social systems'. This linking of the pedagogue to the life of the child and to outside agents connects social pedagogy to the wider environment. The work of Jackson and Smith provides a sense of the way in which social pedagogy can contribute to improving practice in a range of settings with a particular emphasis on residential settings.

In parallel to these developments in Scotland, there was an increasing emphasis on the potential for social pedagogy to improve children's services in England and Wales. In a report for the Department of Education and Skills in 2007, Paget, Eagle and Sitarella produced a paper summarising the possible impact of social pedagogy if introduced into the children's workforce. They suggested that at this time they could not forsee the introduction of social pedagogy as a separate professional discipline. They thought that there was scope for an incremental development of a social pedagogic philosophy and that this would be best supported by facilitating international exchanges.

At the same time the Thomas Coram Research Unit was conducting research into social pedagogy and its impact on children's lives in Denmark, Germany and France.

Their initial research suggested that the key principles of social pedagogy outlined in Chapters 1 to 3, such as head, heart and hands, the three P's and the focus on creativity produced more positive outcomes for young people than equivalent UK based services. They conducted research with pedagogues working in these countries and have produced a substantial body of work supporting their claims. Petrie and Statham (2009) looked at the configuration of social pedagogy across Denmark Germany and France. In Denmark they suggested that social pedagogy was distinguished from social work by the fact that pedagogues focused more on care and child development and that they had more of an emphasis on intervention.

The NCERCC (National Centre for Excellence in Residential Child Care) and SET (the Social Education Trust) pilot study discussed in Chapter 1 gave further impetus to these developments.

Taken together the initial findings were sufficiently positive to prompt the Department for Children and Families to commission a pilot project 'in order to determine the impact of, and best method for, introducing a social pedagogic approach in residential children's homes in line with the *Care Matters* White Paper's commitment' (Cameron et al., 2011: 8). The final report of the project concluded that introducing social pedagogy into the UK would not be a straightforward process. The research designed for this project involved the creation of four comparison groups:

Group One involved homes where continental European qualified pedagogues were already working and in which they would receive support from the project team, but where they had no mandate to promote change in the institution.

Group Two were homes where the intervention was at a higher level. These homes recruited pedagogues from Denmark and Germany who were employed for the two years of the project. They worked within a clear social pedagogic job description.

Group Three was described by TCRU as 'a training model'. Here each of the six residential units recruited to the project would employ two qualified pedagogues who would spend two thirds of their time working with the staff within the units and one third of their time working with the network of services with whom the service intersected.

Group Four was a comparison group which did not employ any social pedagogues.

They noted that although they tested out a number of different approaches to the introduction of social pedagogy, no one method proved entirely appropriate. They suggested that it was possible to distinguish a number of factors which contributed to successful social pedagogic interventions. These included:

- Experience, confidence and skills of social pedagogues.
- Knowledge of social pedagogy among management at all levels and willingness to learn and be challenged.
- Wider support from employer organisation and willingness to invest own resources into training, networking, thinking and reflection.
- Not being wedded to one's own philosophy to the point of exclusion of other ways of thinking.
- Stability of managerial and staff team with commitment to debate and reflect and to live with uncertainty as a positive context for the work.

Cameron et al., 2011: 10–11

Perhaps not surprisingly, this was a slightly more optimistic assessment of the pilot than that produced by the team who were asked to evaluate the project. Berridge et al. (2011: 5) said that the young people within the homes held 'mixed but mainly positive views about the SPs'. Further, they found 'no statistically significant differences in behavioural, emotional or educational outcomes, or in the quality of family contact between the 62 young people who had remained in the pilot or comparison homes' (p. 6). Further, they comment that 'there was no evidence that homes which employed SPs did any better or worse than those which did not' (p. 7). They conclude that for social pedagogy to make an impact in the UK wider systemic changes would need to take place including a movement towards a more highly specialised, highly qualified workforce.

During the period the DCF pilot was running Milligan (2009) produced an evaluation of a project which looked at the possibility of introducing social pedagogy into Scottish residential care. The project was run by Sycamore Services, a residential service with an organisational philosophy based on a humanistic approach to practice and a commitment to working with the child as an individual. The training was undertaken by Sylvia Holthoff and Gabriel Eichsteller at ThemPra (see Chapter 2).

The responses indicated high levels of satisfaction with skills and knowledge development (particularly the understanding they gained of the philosophy around head, heart and hands), the focus on reflection and on personal development – they quote one respondent as saying that 'social pedagogy puts a framework to the work we undertake with children' (Milligan, 2009: 16). Milligan concludes that the training was highly valued by the participants although he notes that it 'was perceived to be congruent with existing Sycamore practice and philosophy' (p. 21). This last point is important as it highlights a consistent issue around organisational buy-in. A lack of conformity around core practice and philosophy may reduce the impact of social pedagogy and indeed seemed to reduce the effectiveness of social pedagogic interventions. The SET/NCERCC and Sycamore interventions, although smaller in scale, seemed to work because of the participants taking on board the social pedagogic approach. The TCRU pilot may not have been so successful because of the inconsistent organisational and management support for the project.

Some evidence for this is provided by the experience of Essex County Council in introducing social pedagogy into their children's residential services. Boyce (2010) described the way the project's objectives were to be met in a variety of ways:

- An initial six-day professional development course run by ThemPra's social pedagogues, introducing residential practitioners to social pedagogic theory and practice.
- Social pedagogy agents: a smaller number of staff in each home have undertaken a further two-day course with ThemPra to enable them to take up lead roles as change agents in their teams in developing social pedagogic practice further. Follow-up support days for social pedagogy agents, run by ThemPra, have taken place to help establish these new roles.
- Accredited written assignments (conferring 30 Level 5 academic credits through the University of Lincoln) based on practitioners' reflective analysis of their efforts to enact social pedagogic theory through creative practical work with children.
- Team-building: ThemPra have undertaken team-building days with whole staff groups in each children's home, focusing on building a pedagogic culture and providing individualised support to teams in making changes to their practice.
- Awareness-raising: a variety of events and meetings have taken place to raise awareness of social pedagogy across children's services in Essex and engage support for the developments in residential services from other professionals, including social workers, independent reviewing officers and CAMHS among others.
- Action research: independent qualitative research to evaluate the impact of the programme from the perspectives of practitioners is being undertaken ... alongside consultation with children and young people on their views of their homes by an internal researcher. This research is ongoing; findings were to be finalised in 2011.
- Strategic implementation framework: a project steering group and an interagency strategic group have been established to lead and oversee the programme. A residential services development officer has been appointed to support the implementation of social pedagogy. A practitioners' network has been set up, providing a bi-monthly meeting space, online discussion forum and quarterly newsletter, for residential workers from across the homes to discuss social pedagogy and have a voice in strategic decision-making.

It was initially reported that the young people in the services reported that they felt as if they were listened to more, are more involved in decisions about their daily lives and have a different range of experiential learning. The staff noted that it introduced 'a more inspiring and inventive approach' and that it 'provides a reminder that our work is with young people, not for or in spite of'. The staff also felt that it offered potential in other work settings.

In their review of what was admittedly their own interventions in Essex, Eichsteller and Holthoff (2012) noted that the interventions by the social pedagogues working in the Essex homes had challenged the perceptions of residential staff by other professionals and suggested that the increased competence and confidence developed by the pedagogues across the three years of the programme was not always appreciated by other professionals. They note the way the pedagogues' relationship with other professionals became reframed as they became more knowledgeable and professionally empowered. They quote one assistant homes manager who said:

> We had an opportunity for a child to have what we believed would be a really positive experience and a great learning opportunity, but we hit a stumbling block when the social worker refused it due to risk! Despite my best efforts to promote this opportunity and evidence how we could manage and reduce the risks it was blocked by the social work team manager. This left the child feeling let down and unheard and me feeling frustrated. After reflecting on this I gathered some evidence from the ThemPra website on risk competence and also attained a . . . (Scottish) . . . study about the detrimental effect risk assessments (if not appropriate!) . . . could have on a child's wellbeing and development. I passed the documents on to the social worker.
>
> (pp. 34–5)

The assistant manager describes how the information was circulated within the social work office and at the time the report was written they were in dialogue with the team manager about the way forward. She concludes by suggesting that:

> . . . social pedagogy is about working in dialogue with other adults as well as children . . . and by using social pedagogy in all that we do we can really begin working in partnership and change practice for the better of our children.
>
> (p. 35)

Cameron et al. (2011) suggest that there are three potential responses to attempts to integrate social pedagogy in residential childcare in the UK. They suggest these were:

- Integration or assimilation into existing theory and practice, such as happened in therapeutic communities.

- Challenge or confrontation where management, staff and organisation practices had the effect of blocking learning.
- Embracing change where mutual and authentic learning was achieved and manifested in new ways of working.

Cameron et al., 2011: 79

Cameron et al. (2011) suggest that for social pedagogy to work, agencies need confidence in the skills and knowledge of pedagogues, organisations need to invest resources into training and networking and should focus on processes of reflection and other ways of working. Finally they suggest that agencies in the UK need to take a critical review of the regulations and procedures surrounding our work with young people and promote debate about alternative ways of working. These conclusions would seem to be consistent with those of NCERCC/SET and with the outcomes anticipated by other writers in this area including Bengtsson et al. (2008) and Hatton (2006, 2008).

Recently, Cameron and Petrie (2011) have looked at how social pedagogy can be utilised in foster care. They suggested that the nature of training for foster carers, with its emphasis on foster carers undertaking short training programmes may produce difficulties in implementing the social pedagogic approach. As noted in Berridge et al.'s (2011) evaluation, social pedagogy works best when there is a commitment to a highly skilled and professional workforce. The current configuration of foster care services would appear to militate against this. However, models such as that employed by Fairway Care in the south of England in which a foster carer lives with a young person who is potentially going to be placed with them may provide a more durable option for introducing a social pedagogic approach.

Cameron and Petrie suggest two possible ways in which social pedagogy could enhance foster care. The first is through a re-written Skills to Foster course which adopted a social pedagogical perspective. The second is to provide a Level 3 type qualification for foster carers which could be a springboard to other educational qualifications. They conclude with a series of recommendations about how social pedagogy could be introduced into foster care and note that there is some enthusiasm for such an approach amongst the people they spoke to.

One area in which social pedagogy can offer some possibilities but which has been dealt with implicitly rather than explicitly in this book, is the area of inter-professional practice. A very recent addition to the research is an evaluation of the Orkney Islands Training Programme undertaken by Vrouwenfelder, Milligan and Merrell (2012). The training was provided by ThemPra and was delivered to 18 staff across education and social care services. One of the participants, a social care professional, suggested that social pedagogy 'refreshes the ideas. It gave us new names for things, and it refreshed the values' (p. 21). The evaluators concluded that 'there is substantial evidence of improved practice and inter-agency working in lines with the principles of social pedagogy'. They further suggested that 'the reflective and experiential elements of the training were fundamental to effectiveness' and that 'changes in organisational design could support (the) . . . processes of 'ripples of change' the participants are currently engaged in' (p. 8). We noted in Chapter 3 how Lyons (2010) argues for the use of creativity across professional areas, and that the early reflections on the Orkney experience suggest that it is not just in a variety of contexts that social pedagogy could make a difference but that in collaborative and inter-professional work social pedagogic approaches could contribute to better practice.

Summary

There are a number of themes running through these evaluations of social pedagogy in relation to children's residential services which can be summarised as:

- Participants enjoy social pedagogic training and feel that it benefits their practice.
- There is some evidence a social pedagogic approach improves the environment of the residential units where it is introduced.
- The young people in the units enjoy the different and often more creative approach.
- To be successful the introduction of social pedagogy into services needs the full commitment of the agency, senior management in particular.
- To achieve this, changes in organisational design and structure need to be implemented.
- Social pedagogy can contribute to the development of professional competence and assertiveness of staff in residential units.
- Social pedagogy can contribute to improved inter-professional practice.

Chapter 8: Social Pedagogy and Youth Work

We have seen in earlier chapters the ways in which the creative and inclusive approach to social pedagogy which is outlined in this book can have beneficial effects in terms of improving the self belief and self confidence of people in a range of different situations. This chapter is concerned with how social pedagogy can in particular improve outcomes for those working within the youth service, or at least what remains of the youth service after the reshaping it has undergone as a result of the dismemberment of public services undertaken by the Coalition government.

Within the last few years the UK has seen the increasing disengagement of young people in a significant number of communities across the UK. Without excusing the actions of those who were involved in these 'riot' situations, early indications also suggest that they can at least partly be explained by young people's sense of dislocation and alienation from mainstream society. A key feature of social pedagogy, as we have seen, has been the re-creation of relationships, an attempt to increase social integration and a commitment to ensuring that the people pedagogues work with engage or re-engage with the communities in which they live. So could a social pedagogic approach to working with young people contribute towards their reintegration into society?

Eichsteller and Rapey (2006) suggested that social pedagogy could play a significant role in reclaiming the core values of youth work. Earlier, Higham (2001) had suggested that the Connexions service, a government funded advice counselling and training service for young people, provided clear opportunities to explore the potential of social pedagogy on young people's lives. The refocusing of the youth service since that period on to more targeted interventions, with the more difficult to reach young people did suggest that there was a possibility of allowing the youth service to reframe its interventions so that social pedagogy could be utilised as a strategy for working with young people.

A report from the Regional Youth Work Unit North East and the University of Sunderland (2010) outlined the conclusions of a six month review of the implications of social pedagogy for youth work. The unit interviewed professionals and young people, and collated information from local authorities carrying out social pedagogy pilot programmes. It was influenced by the *Children's Workforce Strategy*, 2005 and the *Children's Plan* and the 2020 *Children and Young People's Workforce Strategy*. They quote from an article by Oxtoby (2009) which suggested that social pedagogy reflected:

The close and empathetic nature of the social pedagogues' relationship with the young people they work with . . . the social pedagogues can help them to make great strides in terms of developing great life skills.

Oxtoby, 2009, quoted in RWYUNE/UoS, 2010: 6

Respondents to the survey were asked why they did or did not think social pedagogy would benefit children or young people in England. Examples of their responses included.

- *(It) gives direction and support to those young people who, currently, feel dislocated and disconnected from society.*
- *(It has) the ability to effectively communicate with young people and empowers them to make their own informed decisions. The workforce must also recognise that structural aspects impact on young peoples' lived experience of the world and these need to be addressed to ensure sustained change. The workforce must develop skills such as conversation, group work and the recognition of the importance of communication between agencies. It is also imperative to ensure staff are trained and confident in the areas they practice.*
- *Social pedagogy underpins good quality youth work and social work practice, so it is already happening here – we just haven't called it social pedagogy. The key benefit for children and young people is to be regarded as competent individuals who are treated with respect and supported/enabled to learn and develop as they grow into adults.*
- *(It has) much more person centred work or consistent outcomes learning, and deeper understanding of the child and his/her development. However it could lead to dependency on the worker if clarity around boundaries is not good enough.*
- *It depends on which model is introduced. You cannot make integration work by creating one type of worker or one form of knowledge. Integration is dynamic and needs many voices and different knowledge bases.*

RYWUNE/UoS, 2010: 33

As we can see, some of these comments directly connect with the construct of social pedagogy we have been describing throughout the book. The respondents note how it helps people who are dislocated and disconnected gain direction and support, improves communication, helps people make informed decisions and become competent individuals, is person centred and contributes to the integration of service delivery.

The report is notable also for its focus on the views of young people themselves. They point out that young people suggested to them that social pedagogy courses could be beneficial to services in the UK. They suggested that social pedagogy was beneficial in building positive informal relationships, that it enabled professionals to see people in a holistic manner and that it could contribute positively to basic training of all professionals involved with young people (pp. 47–8).

The report also looked at the evaluation of social pedagogy from youth work professionals. One said 'for me the principles of social pedagogy are quite similar to the principles of youth work . . . I think it could really help actually in making our workforce more creative and responsive to young people and their own needs and aspirations' (p. 52). Another respondent commented that 'in terms of young people being influential on what happens to them, not just having things done to them, it will be a really positive thing . . . (in a social pedagogy framework) young people are far more influential in services. And that can only improve services for them because they are the only ones that know what services they need, want and will use' (p. 54).

However a number of the respondents warned about the difficulties of integrating social pedagogy into a different cultural, social and political context. They recognised the possible contribution of social pedagogy but maintained a belief that existing youth work services could meet many of the challenges thrown up by social pedagogy. They quote one area manager of integrated services as saying 'good youth workers have always put the young person at the centre of their work . . . they have the young people helping in terms of planning. They give them choices. They try not to bring their own prejudices into their work . . . good youth work is based on social pedagogy' (p. 56).

The report notes that 46% of professionals who completed their questionnaire believed that social pedagogy would benefit the children and young people's workforce (p. 58). They concluded that social pedagogy could:

- Encourage professionals not to compartmentalise certain aspects of children or young people's lives.
- Provide a more person centred approach.
- Encourage professionals to focus on the views of the children or young person.
- Bring the work force closer together.
- Encourage professionals to take all aspects of a child's life into account (p. 59)

They warned however that amongst the drawbacks to introducing social pedagogy into the UK may be that it is; seen as too idealistic; not sufficiently well understood or effective in a UK context; and not necessarily suitable for all professionals working with children and young people. They commented on what they felt was a lack of understanding of the theory and practice of social pedagogy and an inconsistency in its education and training; problems of funding; the possible dilution of individual specialisms; and the possible resistance of the workforce if proper account was not taken of the cultural differences between the UK and European countries more familiar with the pedagogic tradition. They call for an increased awareness of social pedagogy across the children and young people's workforce, the development of further pilot projects, the review of existing pedagogic training in the UK to ensure consistency across the sector and adequate funding for the development of pedagogy as a profession.

One of the key issues in identifying ways in which social pedagogy can be integrated within youth work is by looking at issues of risk. In *Care Matters* one of the more noticeable responses from young people who were asked their views about the way services meet or fail to meet their needs was that they wished to be heard more. In particular they articulated strong views around issues of risk. The Commission for Social Care Inspection report from 2006 which looked at the views of young people leaving the care system suggested that 'to reach their potential an individual must be allowed – and supported – to take risks, have new experiences and make mistakes' (Hatton, 2008: 16). How then can we align youth work with an approach which can integrate social pedagogy in a positive and beneficial way for young people? A Quartet report from 2009 positively highlighted the ways in which services in Denmark adopted what they regarded as a radically different approach to caring for children and young people which was 'based on nurturing relationships, individuality and creativity' (Gulati and King, 2009: 17)

As we have seen earlier social pedagogy has been characterised as a form of social education and much of the discussion of social pedagogy is formulated through the work of AIEIJ, FESET (Association Européenne des Centres de Formation au Travail Socio-Educatif and the various fora for social educators which make up FESET). The Nordic Forum for Social Educators (NFSE) argue that:

> *Social education is the theory about how psychological, social and material conditions and various value orientations encourage or prevent the general development and growth, life quality and welfare of the individual of the group.*
> NFSE, 2003: 8

The NFSE suggests that central to social education processes are issues of integration and that the general aim is to ensure the integration of excluded and marginalised people. Their focus is on working in ways which ensure the people they engage with benefit from rather than become dependent on the services they use. This they suggest is achieved through them connecting 'critical analysis with constructive actions' (p. 10). At the core of social education work is the notion of becoming reflective practitioners:

> ... *social educators in the Nordic countries work within many various fields, differing from one country to the other. The Norwegian childcare workers, barnevernpedagoger, perform tasks and functions that are to some extent similar to a social worker in Denmark and Sweden. In Sweden there a few social*

educators compared to social workers. In contrast to their Danish colleagues, Swedish social workers perform direct social educational treatment work . . . in Denmark as well as in the Faroe Islands and Greenland, the education is a common social education programme that is also aimed at taking care of children and young people in day-care, schools and leisure time facilities.

NFSE, 2003: 11

This conceptualisation of social education suggests a way of realigning youth work in the UK to incorporate perspectives which move beyond risk maintenance or risk management, which has often been the impact of government intervention. This has often been against the wishes of youth workers and their agencies, particularly, but not only, those in the non-statutory sector. This chapter will conclude with a brief look at two potential ways of achieving this, and at some examples drawn from international practice.

Postive youth development

The author is not suggesting that these more challenging approaches have been absent from developments in youth work in the UK. What is being suggested is that over the last ten years we have seen developments within youth work which have been akin to those in other sectors of the welfare state. These include a focus on young people as problematic rather than them as people with capacity. We have seen the growth of organisations such as youth parliaments and through Care Matters and Youth Matters recognition of the importance of listening to and engaging with young people. Yet this has been increasingly against a backdrop in which young people have been, and continue to be, seen as a threat, rather than a resource within our societies. As we saw in earlier chapters social pedagogy can help us reframe debates so that we focus on the creativity of young people, their capacity to act (and in a positive rather than negative way) and the importance of including, engaging with and promoting young people as active citizens. Recent foci within UK youth work on targeted interventions with the most vulnerable young people, while important, can result in us reinforcing negative images of young people rather than the positive outcomes which social pedagogy, and the more affirmative youth work models known as positive youth development and community youth development can help attain.

The idea of positive youth development has emerged over the last two decades. Flanagan, Syvertsen and Wray-Lake (2007) suggest that positive youth development is, in a similar way to the strengths perspective in social work, an attempt to focus on young people's assets and not their deficits. They suggest that this approach can be extended by recognising young people as agents of change and that political activism should be seen as an important element in such positive youth development. To achieve this, they argue, that we would need to legitimise marginalised identities (a similar point made by Bill Jordan (2006) in his work on poverty and social exclusion). They argue also that we should support young people in contesting race and class inequalities in a wide range of welfare services including public spaces (this would mean developing a much more resistant discourse to the paradigms which problematise young people such as ASBOs and dispersal orders).

Further, they put forward the idea that young people are currently, and will continue to be, involved in environmental and global justice activism. Finally they argue that young people can be encouraged to critically analyse the societies around them. They suggest that 'with the proper knowledge and skills, youth can move beyond individual acts of service and link their sense of social responsibility to constructive political action' (p. 251)

Community youth development

A similar approach is suggested by Perkins, Borden and Villarruel (2001: 43) when they talk about community youth development, a further attempt to develop the positive youth development model. They suggest that community youth development 'shifts the emphasis from a dual focus of youth being problem free and fully prepared, to a triadic focus for youth being problem free, fully prepared and engaged partners. More importantly, this focus recognises that there is an interdependent relationship between positive and healthy youth outcomes and positive and healthy communities'. They suggest that at the core of community youth development is a focus on the young person's capacity to both understand and act upon the environment, a recognition that this involves the active support of people across the community, and that central to this is the engagement of youth in 'constructive and challenging activities that build their competence and foster supported relationships with peers and with adults' (p. 48). Finally they suggest that to achieve these goals requires developments in youth participation and partnerships with their community.

Support for these contentions is provided by the National Youth Agency in the report cited earlier. They suggest that:

> These positive role models and 'word of mouth' recommendations of projects by other users are powerful tools for engagement, adding authenticity to the work through shared experience.
>
> National Youth Agency, 2009: 3

International examples

An example of how such an approach can be developed is provided by a youth worker at the Blaeksprutten (Octopussy) youth project in Copenhagen (Hatton, 2001b – the project is part of the SSP model widely used in Denmark – see Langager, 2009). This is a project which focused on the experience of a poor, marginalized community with a high proportion of black and minority young people living within its boundaries. The project aimed to break down the barriers between the police, social welfare agencies and local young people. The project leader said of the project's approach, that they seek to provide the young people using the project with an increased sense of self-worth.

One of the project workers at Blaekspruten describes how:

> *When we give these kids more confidence and a strong identity they go out on the streets and in social society and can be like normal people, they do not have to be afraid and do not have to pretend to be tough guys, because they know from the inside that they are good enough. After giving these kids self-confidence they can do more things for other kids and adults in social society. We are showing the social society that the kids around here are OK.*

Hatton, 2001b

A Project Leader at Blaekspruten demonstrates the problems people often face when they try to explain the nature of their difficulties to people in agencies, including social care agencies:

> *A woman is living with a man in a family together, he is violent towards her. Whenever it happens she goes to some social assistants who really pity her. They say, 'I feel really sorry for you'. She says that is not what she needs. She needs someone to cry out and say 'do something about it. Rise up and do something yourself'. The system does not really handle the problem, we do not really involve ourselves, we just listen.*

Hatton, 2001b

Aluffi-Pentini and Lorenz (1996) pointed to the importance of social professionals, including youth workers and social pedagogues, challenging structural as well as individual oppression when addressing racism when they describe the challenge faced by Italian youth and social workers who felt that ' racism was a challenge to educators in all parts of the country, that all pedagogical interventions had to be embedded in a clear political analysis, that cultural differences reflected power differentials' (p. vi).

In France the social pedagogic tradition is not so developed but social professionals adopt social education and animation methods (animateur) to work with marginalised and excluded youth, particularly in the Banlieu (Ott, 2011). Hurstel (2012) says, in any integration projects, for interventions with young people to be successful they need to link together the social and cultural. As part of Banlieues Europe he suggests the need to utilise cultural activities to animate young people to promote social change.

This is particularly important at a time when racist discourses are being mainstreamed in contemporary politics (UKREN, 2006) and is apposite in the light of earlier discussions about the importance of creativity to any new forms of practice.

Participation and young people

This means engaging with young people and ensuring their participation in all levels of decision-making. The United Nation's Children's Fund (2001: 9–11) suggested that participation had a number of important values for young people. These included;

- Participation as a human right and thus something beneficial in its own right.
- Participation as being critical to self development.
- As a way of building effectiveness and sustainability, particularly where they are fully involved, or even the authors of a project.
- It demonstrates that young people can make a real contribution to society.
- It fosters learning, builds life skills and enables self-protection. They refer in particular to the way young people 'will be better equipped to deal with abusive, threatening or unfair situations because they will be in a better position to seek advice, exit a harmful situation when necessary or cope creatively when there is no exit'.

(p. 10)

They quote the Dominican Youth Group who argue that 'participation implies decision making and is viewed as a strategy for human development as it is closely linked to the promotion of leadership (with transforming capacities) at the social level, that empowers adolescents, adolescent groups, communities, provinces, and the country to get involved in the processes towards individual and collective development' (p. 12).

The relevance of social pedagogy to this view of youth work is illustrated by Vaisanen (2010) when he talks about the way social pedagogy's main focus is on the integration of displaced young people into society. This can be achieved, he argues, through dialogue which 'implies an equal role of young people and adults in interactions aimed to solve problems of commitment to education . . . Paying respect to subjectivity and the rights of self-determination of young people leads to helping them to identify and clarify their own targets' (Vaisanen, 2010: 28).

This view of work with young people as potentially empowering at a structural as well as an individual level takes us to an understanding of social pedagogy as an activity which needs to engage with social change as well as individual development. This suggests that the agenda in our work with young people needs to reclaim the radical youth practices of participation and inclusion, and should be oriented towards social action rather than focusing on young people as a problem which needs to be solved or fixed. A bridge between these two approaches can be seen in the links between community development and social pedagogy which the author explores later in this book (see also Hatton, 2012b).

Summary

This chapter demonstrated how social pedagogy can be applied beyond children's residential services to work with marginalised young people. It drew on work done with young people using a social pedagogic approach and suggested that such work can be enhanced if integrated with positive youth development, community development and participatory approaches. It concluded with a look at international examples of how such an approach could work.

Exercise

Do you agree with the suggestion that social pedagogy could play a significant role in reclaiming the core values of youth work?

What do you understand those core values to be and how do you think they could be supported by a social pedagogic approach?

Chapter 9: Personalisation, Adult Social Care and Social Pedagogy

So far discussions on social pedagogy in the UK are focused almost exclusively on its potential to secure better outcomes for children in residential services. However, as can be seen by the edited collections by Kornbeck and Rosendal-Jensen (2009) and Gustavsson, Hermansson and Hämäläinen (2003), social pedagogy in Europe has a much wider focus than this. This chapter looks at its implications for people with disabilities and in particular the personalisation agenda, which is currently attracting a lot of interest. Gardner has commented positively on Higham's assertion that social work should be seen as having a holistic quality which enables 'social workers to practice in a range of situations, with a range of different people, and to be open to developing new roles' (Gardner, 2011: 115). This chapter seeks to demonstrate how organisations and individuals working with people with disabilities can embrace a social pedagogic approach to improve the life experience of people using such services. It seeks to demonstrate that the principles of personalisation can be linked to a social pedagogic approach.

Personalisation

Personalisation has been defined as 'starting with the person as an individual with strengths, preferences and aspirations and putting them at the centre of the process of identifying their needs and making choices about how and when they are supported to live their lives. It requires a significant transformation of adult social care so that all systems, processes, staff and services are geared up to put people first' (Carr, 2010). The Department of Health has argued that personalisation should be seen across the adult social care sector. It says 'it is about better support more tailored to individual choices and preferences in all care settings' (DoH, 2008a: 5 quoted in Carr, 2010: 4).

At the core of personalisation is the provision to people using adult services of personal budgets. Carr shows that this is not an insignificant element of services as approximately 115,000 adults over 18 in England were receiving a personal budget, representing 6.5% of all adults using services in 2008/9. Central to the idea of personal budgets is the notion that there should be transparency to both providers and service users in the level of money available to meet their individuals care needs.

Carr argues that personalisation encapsulates core social work values. It was first outlined in the Prime Minister's Strategy Unit report *Building on Progress: Public Services* (2007). The report describes personalisation as representing a vision of how 'the state should empower citizens to shape their own lives and the services they receive' (Prime Minister's Strategy Unit, 2007: 33 quoted in Carr, 2010: 17). The application of personalisation to adult social care was further developed in *Putting People First* (HM Government, 2007) and is consistent with the government white paper *Strong and Prosperous Communities* (DfCLG, 2006).

The government outlined its strategy for adult social care in *Working to Put People First* (2009), which argued that there was a need for a cultural shift in the delivery of services which was characterised by a move from:

- Clients to citizens.
- Welfare to well being.
- Expert to enabling.
- Transactional change to transformational change.
- Safety net to spring board.

DoH, 2009: 17

At the centre of this new agenda is the emphasis on joint and integrated working between social, health care and other services including housing and employment services. This commitment is underpinned by a number of key principles described by Carr (2010) as the Seven Common Core Principles for Self Care (determined by *Skills for Care* and *Skills for Health*). They include commitments to:

- Ensure individuals are able to make informed choices to manage their self care needs.
- Communicate effectively to enable individuals to assess their needs and develop and gain confidence to self care.
- Support and enable individuals to access appropriate information to manage their self care needs.
- Support and enable individuals to develop skills in self care.
- Support and enable individuals to use technology to support self care.
- Advise individuals how to access support networks and participate in the planning, development and evaluation of services.
- Support and enable risk management and risk taking to maximise independence and choice.

DoH, 2009: 44

There is a significant emphasis within *Working to Put People First* on developing workforce capacity both in terms of career pathways and workforce development. The report calls for an increase in the number of social care apprenticeships including apprenticeships for personal assistants to facilitate the personalisation agenda. The strategy talks about improving the image of the social care sector workforce so that it is seen as one 'which offers many opportunities – a variety of different careers, all drawn together with a common purpose of working with adults in social care settings'

(p. 28). It goes on to say 'we aspire to a future with an increasing prevalence of people using services and carers who help design and implement recruitment programmes as a way to ensure that the right people with the right aptitude, skills and talent can be attracted and retained in the sector' (p. 28). This final comment has a particular resonance for those interested in introducing social pedagogy into the wider social care workforce.

The emphasis on inclusion and 'aptitude, skills and talent' are consistent with the vision of social pedagogy outlined in earlier chapters. This is also consistent with Local Authority Circular (DH, 2008) which says that the personalisation agenda is about 'every person across the spectrum of need, having choice and control over the shape of his or her support, in the most appropriate setting. For some, exercising choice and control will require a significant level of assistance either through professionals or through independent advocates' (LAC/DoH, 2008: 2). Underpinning this is the belief that 'the shared ambition is to meet the aspiration to put people first through a radical reform of public services. It will mean that people are able to live their own lives as they wish, confident that services are of high quality, are safe and promote their own individual requirements for independence, well-being and dignity.'

The seven core principles outlined above were developed in consultation with people who use adult social care services and their carers. There are significant areas of consistency between these principles and the work of social pedagogues and social educators. Carr (2010) points out social workers in the UK can also draw on skills of counselling and community development to take forward the personalisation agenda. The latter are particularly important if we are to realise the inclusion agenda which is at the heart of personalisation.

Co-production

A way of linking these approaches together can be found in the new 'co-production agenda'. At the heart of this agenda is an emphasis on user-led organisations (Ramsden, 2010). Co-production was defined in the Department of Health's *Personalisation Communications Toolkit* in the following way:

> *Co-production is when you as an individual influence the support and services you receive, or when groups of people get together to influence the way that services are designed, commissioned and delivered.*
>
> PPF Communications Toolkit quoted in Ramsden, 2010

Ramsden also quotes In Control who describe co-production as:

> *. . . to produce together. Almost everything that professionals can attempt to do to help others can be better thought of as co-production. Co-production*

promises better outcomes by attending to the partnership that is necessary between the citizen and the professional in order to achieve these outcomes.
cited in Ramsden, 2010: 8

Needham and Carr (2009: 12) argue, in their evidence review of co-production, that an essential feature of co-production is the focus on people using services as experts in their own requirements. They suggest that co-production activities promote mutual aid, involve the broader community and redefine the notion of outcomes in public services moving from the quantifiable to the less quantifiable aspects of care such as, 'befriending, building relationships and broader quality of life issues'. Interestingly they point to how some initiatives can develop 'practical skills . . . such as DIY skills' and promoting social capital through 'building supportive relationships and increasing personal self-confidence and activity' (p. 13).

Such approaches clearly resonate with the elements of the pedagogic relationship mentioned earlier, particularly the 'hand' and the 'heart'.

The principles of the 'common third' map very well against the aspirations of the personalisation and co-production agendas. The 'common third' is about working in partnership, with the social pedagogue and the user of services developing a subject-subject relationship which recognises the strengths and capabilities of each party and which seeks to produce beneficial outcomes through processes of interaction and the minimisation of power differentials. Personalisation and co-production fit very well within the *CRISP* philosophy outlined in Chapter 4. The *CRISP* approach can enhance personalisation and co-production by emphasising not only the inclusion elements of the relationship but also the creative elements. We have seen in the chapter on creativity and pedagogy (Chapter 4) the way in which a focus on creativity can enhance outcomes for people experiencing a wide variety of often negative experiences. Such an approach to personalisation, co-production and social pedagogy will need to be underpinned by the discourses around power outlined in Chapter 5.

The recognition in this chapter of the importance of risk taking and risk promotion is also consistent with a social pedagogic approach. Hatton (2008) has shown how there has been a consistent theme in the consultations around *Every Child Matters*, *Our Health, Our Care, Our Say* and *Independence, Well-being and Choice*, let alone the personalisation and co-production discussions outlined above, that people using services have a strong desire to have their voices heard. As part of this a key message that emerges from all of these consultations is that people resent the paternalism inherent in many current forms of social care/social work practice. They want to be able to take risks, make choices and participate fully in any care services that they receive.

Social economy and social cooperatives

A further way in which the agenda for people with disabilities and the social pedagogic approach could be linked together is through a focus on social economy and social cooperatives. Hermansson (2003: 47) says that the adoption of such an approach could transform the way society views people with disabilities. He argues that a focus on social cooperatives means that:

> *Participants . . . should take responsibility for and operate the services that they receive, which in turn explains why an underlying pedagogical approach is a distinctive feature of such projects.*

He sees this as an empowering process through which the participant's social capital is significantly increased leading to a 'growth in personal power and self reliance' (p. 57). Interestingly he characterises the institutions utilising this approach as ones with significant creative environments which 'promote communication between different groups and so strengthen the individual potential for autonomous action' (pp. 49–50). Such a model is consistent with the theoretical model *CRISP* outlined in Chapter 4 and developed through the discussion of power discourses in Chapter 5.

In light of the above it would seem that adult social care could benefit significantly from the adoption of a social pedagogic approach. We have seen in earlier chapters how the social pedagogic approach has improved outcomes for young people in residential care. It is likely that the adoption of such an approach would also improve outcomes for adults in a range of settings including residential and institutional care.

This is borne out by a small-scale piece of action research undertaken with young people with learning difficulties by Carter et al. (2012). They used Petrie's framework for understanding social pedagogy to carry out a small evaluative study into how young people with learning difficulties responded to the use of social pedagogy in a small group (six young people) who accessed a family link or short break setting. They undertook a range of activities with the young people utilising the head, heart and hands pedagogic approach discussed earlier. They specifically utilised this approach because they felt that the three elements within the approach, particularly the emphasis on hands (creativity), ensured a greater level of involvement from the young people than approaches which demanded greater cognitive skills. They noted how the young people became increasingly involved in the group (even those who previously had difficulty engaging with others) and found that:

> *Social pedagogy enhances involvement by providing a liberating space for the young person to reveal more about themselves, their hopes and aspirations, and thus what families, friends and services should be providing for them.*
>
> Carter et al., 2012: 6

In common with earlier findings around residential services for young people they found that 'the closer the group's experience came to accepted precepts of social pedagogy, the more successful the session was perceived' (p. 6). They conclude that 'social pedagogy promotes involvement within a policy framework of person-centred planning and personalised services' (p. 7).

Although small in nature the research by Carter et al. would seem to support the central premise of the book that social pedagogy has a wider applicability within UK social professional practice than has so far been explored. The relevance of social pedagogy appears to be further enhanced if it is linked to an inclusion agenda and if it promotes partnership and equality between the parties engaged in the pedagogic process. The AIEJI (2010) argue that central to good practice with people with (developmental) disabilities is a recognition of the importance of power relations and that social educational practice should have as its aim 'providing the individual person . . . the opportunity to realise his or her rights and to be included in the community of society through self-determination and participation.' They go on to say that:

> The participation of people with developmental disabilities must go further than just . . . daily activities. The concept must be understood as the citizen's influence on the community. The person must experience that he or she can contribute in many different contexts . . . it is the role of the social educator to support the individual in having as much influence as possible while ensuring their representation and participation.
>
> AIEJI, 2010: 21

Summary

This analysis is consistent with the concept of social pedagogy outlined in Chapters 4 and 5. The key elements of a social pedagogic approach to working with people with disabilities can be summarised as:

- A focus on inclusion, participation and rights.
- The development of services which promote relationships and which emerge through a partnership between the pedagogue/social worker/service provider and the user of the services.
- The integration of a co-production approach into social pedagogy.
- Engagement with alternative forms of service provision including social enterprises and social cooperatives.

Exercise

How could the seven core aims of the personalisation agenda and the concept of co-production be supplemented by a social pedagogic approach? Apply your conclusions to:

(a) Older people and their carers.

(b) Young people who experience learning difficulties.

Chapter 10: Community and Pedagogy

In the UK current debates around social welfare are driven by the Coalition government's ideas on the 'Big Society', with a focus on localism, empowerment and social action. These form part of what is claimed to be a process of decentralizing power so that communities can take control of their own affairs. As the architect of the 'Big Society', David Cameron said when launching the policy, 'You can call it liberalism. You can call it empowerment, you can call it freedom, you can call it responsibility. I call it the Big Society' (Prime Minister David Cameron: 19th July 2010 cited in McCabe, 2010). Anna Coote of the New Economics Foundation says of the 'Big Society' that it 'shifts responsibility from the state to individuals and families, and from public services to self-help, charity, local enterprise and global commerce . . . It is also a bid to replace paid with unpaid labour on a massive scale' (Coote: 2012). The reality is that rather than promoting a radical agenda the policy is characterised by the promotion of neo-liberal policies, including increased privatisation of welfare, a rolling back of the state and a reduction in public spending (Jordan, 2011).

Lavalette and Woodward (2007) quote Andrew Glyn who characterises neo-liberalism as being about:

> *Low inflation, quiescent industrial relations, freedom for capital to chase profitable opportunities without restraint and the domination of market based solutions.*
>
> Glyn, 2006: viii quoted in Lavalette and Woodward, 2007: 36

For social professionals neo-liberalism means the privatisation of welfare and health services, attacks on the professionalism and status of welfare workers, significant cuts in services, accompanied often by attacks on the poor and demonisation of groups of marginalised people such as the young and unqualified, people with disabilities, single parents etc.

Perhaps not surprisingly colleagues across Europe see reports from the UK and conclude that UK community work is driven by this neo-liberal agenda and is therefore inherently conservative by nature. Yet, the UK has a history of radical community and social work. Attention has recently refocused on the lessons that can be learned from a re-examination of community work and community action during the period from the early 1970s to the early 1990s (Ferguson and Woodward, 2009; Hatton, 2008: 12). By drawing on this tradition we can begin to reframe the Coalition's proposals around localism and social action as has been suggested by Purcell (2012: 273). He argues that 'in any everyday activity lies an abundance of opportunities for ordinary people to subvert the rituals and representations that institutions seek to impose on them: in effect to remake part of the world in their personal interest'. This raises similar issues as the discussions around Weedon's development of the idea of 'reverse discourse' in Chapter 5. The 1970s and 1980s were interesting times for community work and radical community action and illustrate the point Purcell is making (see in particular Bolger et al., 1982; Craig et al., 1982). Fleetwood and Lambert (1982: 48) reflected on the difficulties of developing a radical socialist community work practice:

> *Trying to maintain a socialist commitment and an engagement in community action in the 1970s was like walking in shoes soled with banana skins: the weight of orthodox socialist theory shot a leg sliding one way whilst the experience and evolving practice of community action sent the other leg in the opposite direction.*

These comments remain apposite today. The regulatory framework within which much welfare practice took place in the years since 1997 often constrained the possibilities for more radical practice. However organisations such as the Social Work Action Network have sought to revitalise radical discourses and draw on the radical social and community work traditions of the 1970s and 1980s (see the SWAN website www.swan.org; Hatton, 2001a; and Ferguson and Woodward, 2009). How then can we learn from the past, recognising the strengths of earlier theory and practice yet also subjecting it to critical analysis?

Part of the reason for the new direction in social welfare we have seen over the last ten years (the development of initiatives outside the state sector) is the belief that a focus on community and localism is consistent with an inclusive approach. This is reflective of the way in which New Labour, when it came to power in 1997, sought to promote a more inclusive sense of community. Some writers have seen this attempt to re-craft the idea of community as a fundamental concept in New Labour's ideology.

Fremeaux (2005: 267) argues that this was seen as a counterpoint to hierarchical and centralised policies and was an attempt to 'invoke the capacity of the community to revitalise and regenerate local areas' (Fremeux, 2005).

Morison (2000: 105) saw evidence of an 'increasing involvement by the voluntary sector in delivering a whole range of services'. He noted how the voluntary sector had been estimated to account for 1 in 25 of the workforce, with a total contribution to the economy of £25 billion per annum. Clearly the sector is not therefore an insignificant part of the welfare environment in the UK. Bateman drew attention to how important the voluntary sector is, for instance on the development of welfare advice services (Bateman, 2006).

In March 2004 an international conference brought together community workers, community groups and policy makers to look at how community development could contribute to the development of civil society. The outcome was a common statement on community development in Europe which was known as the Budapest declaration (Craig, Gorman & Vercseg, 2004: 2) They defined community development as:

> *A way of strengthening civil society by prioritising the actions of communities, and their perspective in the development of social, economic and environmental policy.*
>
> Craig, Gorman & Vercseg, 2004: 423–9

A key factor around contemporary debates about welfare practice has been in the central focus that statutory social work plays in current practice. Attempts to characterise social work as an activity which takes place in the statutory sector provide an inaccurate account of the way contemporary social work is heading. Qualified social workers still tend to gravitate toward working in local authorities, whether in the children's or adult workforce or multi-disciplinary initiatives such as Youth Offending Teams or Community Mental Health teams, but there is more than anecdotal evidence to suggest that a significant number of graduates are choosing to work in non-statutory settings. The recent General Social Care Council report *Raising Standards* points to the large number of graduates employed in social care/services work but fails to indicate whether this means they are statutory or voluntary agencies (GSCC, 2008: xi-xii). Yet public discussions around social work continue to take this narrow view of the work social workers undertake. This underplays or ignores much of the more innovative practice that is taking place outside these sectors and that can be found in the voluntary and independent sectors (Hatton: 2008, Chapter 6; Stepney and Popple, 2008).

However, we need to beware of sentimentalising the community and voluntary sectors, which can also be appropriated to project neo-liberal values. This can be seen in particular in the attempts to promote social enterprise as the way forward. The National Strategy for Neighbourhood Renewal report on *Enterprise and Social Exclusion* (1999: 107) suggested that social enterprises were important because they could play a key part in tackling social exclusion, arguing that, social enterprises can build 'human and social capital . . . (and) strengthen local communities'. They identified one of the main problems facing social enterprises as sustainability in that there needed to be embedded support mechanisms so that they could draw down finance from various sectors of government. They went on to argue that social enterprises differ from private sector businesses in that 'they are geared towards social regeneration and help, rather than simply the generation of profits. As such they do not fall within the standard definitions of private or public sector enterprises' (p. 105). Indeed the Budapest declaration referred to above also refers to the need for the EU to encourage the networking and their role as 'active and legitimate partners in the development of local communities' (Craig et al.: 5).

Social enterprises

Could then a focus on social enterprises, and the underpinning belief in social entrepreneurship, provide a way of making services more accountable and relevant to the people who use them? Social enterprises tap into a core belief within social and community work that we should support people to take action to empower themselves and their communities. They appear to provide a third way between the state and private welfare which can allow people to engage with processes of change, take risks and achieve levels of self development. To this extent they provide a challenge to the more moribund and procedural focus still found in too much contemporary social and community work. They relate to the changing structure of welfare in that they are a clear expression that the mixed economy of welfare does not necessarily mean an increase in managerialism or central control but that it can provide a way of allowing local people and communities to generate their own solutions to their problems.

The focus on the entrepreneur can be seen to mirror some of the ideas in the more radical approaches to social and community work which postulate the way in which community leaders can emerge organically from the local community (Gramsci, 1972; Freire, 1972) (see Chapter 5). But do they? Instead they would appear to remain a clear expression of a neo-liberal agenda. They promote the idea of the powerful and charismatic leader who creates profits for reinvestment in the community. Profits, entrepreneurship and lack of accountability do not suggest a future for social and community work which many of us would wish to see.

However a focus on community development's potential as a transformatory strategy highlights an approach to empowerment which could have taken, and could still take, community work forward. It may also suggest a way in which the local state can be encouraged to fund 'critical organisations of poor people' (Byrne, 1989).

By taking account of what Marynowicz-Hetka (2007) calls the 'transversalism' of social pedagogy it may be possible to reconstitute community development. She attributes transversalism as constructing a broad social movement which integrates issues of race, class, gender and community, which may be able to overturn the more pessimistic analysis.

Community development and social pedagogy

Eriksson (2011) has pointed to the differences and similarities between community development and social pedagogy. The former she attributes to their differing origins (community development as a way of thinking, social pedagogy as a way of doing), to the geographical spaces they occupy (European as against Anglo-Saxon), to the differing welfare regimes in which they operate, and to way in which social pedagogy can be formulated as an individual intervention while community development is by definition a collective response to the problems people face. However she argues that there are clear similarities. Both provide a holistic understanding of education, development and learning. She suggests that in both traditions, there is 'a tension between a radical and a conservative side' and that they both raise the question of whether the individual, society or both should be the focus of change (2011: 414–17).

Lone (2010: 62) raises similar issues when discussing the use of treatment collectives in residential care for people who misuse substances. She argues that because of the lack of hierarchy in these agencies there has been a 'strong and radical political bias' which has allowed them to provide an alternative social pedagogy to the medicalised services available elsewhere in Norway. This, she argues, is partly to do with skepticism in Norway towards all kinds of residential care and quotes Edle Ravndal who in a review of the working of collectively organised services suggests that:

> *The collective model seems still to defend its place as an important component in a larger treatment system for the most challenged youths.*
>
> Lone, 2010: 70

Social pedagogy and community development therefore appear to share the potential to transform people's experience and create new ways of delivering and experiencing welfare services. They can connect with traditions whose focus has been on promoting change, not merely on ameliorating the impact of inequality and disadvantage (Hatton, 2008, 2012). It is worth remembering the words of the authors of *In and Against the State* who noted 'Our struggle is therefore in part the assertion of our own ways of doing things, ways which are rooted in people's lived experience rather than betraying it, ways that strengthen rather than whittle away people's confidence, and foster collectivity rather than individualism' (p. 53).

This emphasis asserts the right of people to be involved in transforming and recreating their own situations. It also suggests that community development, with its emphasis on precisely such re-creative practice may have a continuing validity in Britain. Although in the UK we now face a neo-liberal government intent on dismantling the state and paradoxically forcing us to look to altruism rather than state sponsorship for funding, we have the opportunity to reclaim the language of localism, social action and empowerment which was central to radical community work (and which we can see in some of the social pedagogic discourses discussed above). This will involve utilising a reverse discourse (Foucault, 1980; Weedon, 1989) which reclaims the language of community, localism and social action from the neo-liberals and uses it to promote the empowerment of the marginalised and excluded. Social pedagogy, particularly if combined with a community development perspective, can contribute to such developments

Summary

This chapter looked at the ways social pedagogy can contribute to community development. It looked at how community development can provide an alternative to a narrow neo-liberal welfare agenda by placing a focus on social transformation.

Exercise

Social pedagogy is often characterised as an approach which is based on relations between individuals. How can social pedagogy contribute to a new vision of community work and social action?

Part Four: Social Pedagogy for the UK

Chapter 11: Social Pedagogy and The Challenge to Social Work and Social Care

Social work in the UK is at an interesting juncture in its development as a profession. The final report from the Social Work Task Force and the subsequent work of the Social Work Reform Board suggested the need to refocus social work so that it became a more clearly defined profession. There was a recognition that social work had become far too instrumental and procedural in its focus and that it was necessary to build a clear professional identity for social work. The highly critical nature of earlier analysis of the failures of social work such as the Climbié enquiry, the Laming report, the further enquiry of Baby Peter and the following Laming Report had seen social work as a profession subject to virulent critiques from media, politicians and other professionals. The establishment of the Task Force and subsequently the Reform Board were attempts to revitalise social work.

The Social Work Reform Board's final report *Building a Safe and Confident Future* (2011) argued for changes in the way that social workers were educated, in the processes of continuous professional development and in the way that organisations who employed social workers should develop in future. Among these changes, which have now been taken on by The College of Social Work, was the establishment of a Professional Capability Framework (2012) which would provide a means of developing the practice and education of social workers from their first entry into social work education degree programmes through to their employment as senior professionals. For the purposes of this analysis, the key elements of the professional capability framework's nine domains were the focus on developing professionalism, professional leadership, diversity and ethics, and economic well being. These are part of the attempt to refocus social work so that it became more service user and carer focused and that it reclaimed its original vision with its focus on relationships and well being. Ruch, Turney and Ward (2010) have suggested that this is precisely what is needed if we are going to work towards a new welfare settlement. As they have suggested:

> *Working in and with relationships is emotionally demanding and frequently time consuming. Even if the encounter itself is short lived . . . it requires a level of engagement, openness and willingness to commit something of one's self. Maintaining relationships through time can be immensely satisfying and*

sustaining for the participants, but, again, this does not come without effort and
. . . working with extremes of emotion can be extremely challenging.

Turney, Ward and Ruch, 2010: 244–5

There is considerable anxiety about the future direction in which we are heading. This is partly because of the poor press social work received as a result of Baby Peter and the perception that social workers had not learned sufficient lessons, or made sufficient improvements in their practice, in the time between the Climbié inquiry and this more recent tragedy. However, with the decision to appoint the Social Work Task Force to consider the future direction of social work some of the more irrational and biased media criticism dissipated. In their joint ministerial letter to social workers Ed Balls and Alan Johnson referred to the fact that the role of social workers 'is critical to the nation' and that among social workers 'there is real appetite for positive change'. While many social workers would share these sentiments they are also keen to know in what direction that change is heading.

Since the Task Force began many social workers, from across the spectrum, have engaged with debates about the direction in which social work should progress. Lord Laming reported on the lessons still to be learned after Climbié and Baby Peter and, among other issues, recommended the development of a national strategy, improved leadership and accountability within the profession, increased support for children, improved interagency working, the development of a national children's social work strategy and the protection of budgets for the staffing and training of child protection services (Laming, 2009).

The Task Force presented its interim report in July 2009 and reported that:

- Social work as a profession is not as attractive as some others and this is compounded by staffing shortages.
- 'Arrangements for education, training and career progression are not producing – or retaining – enough social workers suited to the full demands of frontline practice' (Social Work Task Force, 2009: 7).
- Social work needs to be able to demonstrate its effectiveness and as a result 'the distinct role of social workers in modern public services is unclear' (Social Work Task Force, 2009: 7).

Almost simultaneously the Department of Children, Schools, and Families Select Committee reported on the training of social workers and expressed some concern about what they called 'the plethora of new initiatives which have been set in motion before the Task Force reports' (DCSF, 2009: 3). They note the disparity between Higher Education Institutions' (HEIs') and employers' expectations of what should be expected of qualifying social workers and pointed to the importance of a 'substantial injection of resources into frontline social work capacity (which) will in the long term enable the changes in training and professional development we have outlined' (DCSF, 2009: 12). These proposals were reinforced by the recommendations of the Munro Review (2010 – and the earlier work around the *Reclaiming Social Work* agenda) which also drew attention to the need to refocus social work on the needs of service users/carers and to re-emphasise the importance of relationships and professional judgement in social work interventions. Unfortunately although the Coalition has continued to support the developments coming out of the Task Force, Reform Board and Munro, additional resources promised have not materialised and are unlikely to do so in the current climate of austerity.

A number of common themes can be discerned in these discussions:

- A justifiable concern at the need to protect vulnerable young people.
- A recognition of the need for social work to develop a voice which can articulate this need for a recognition of the difficult job social workers undertake.
- A need for greater investment in social work and surrounding services (although it was noticeable that in all public discussions involving the Task Force resources were the issue which was sidelined).

These are interesting developments and can allow for hope of a more positive future for social work. However they are underpinned by a number of factors of which we should be wary. There is a danger, with the possible exception of the DCSF report, that they present an almost hegemonic belief that employers are the best people to drive forward change. They promote inter-professional or collaborative practice but are not clear on how this would operate. Is it collaboration between equals or a reflection of the old political maxim 'primus inter pares' – first among equals? Too often social work has been the secondary partner in such arrangements. How can social workers ensure that this is not the case in the future? The reports say very little about the values which underpin social work and of the importance of social workers engaging with people who use services if they are to be effective in meeting the needs of the people with whom they interact. Furthermore, they are almost wholly predicated on the belief that social work only takes place in statutory settings and their focus is often on service delivery – the task of social work, rather than the way we think about and develop our work – the theory underpinning what we do. Finally their narrowness of focus fails to take into account what we could learn from other countries about how best social work services should be delivered (Lawrence and Lyons, 2008; Askegaard and Payne, 2010).

We need to ask if there is an alternative vision that we can articulate which provides a way forward which is consistent with the humanistic and existentialist principle which brought many of us into social work in the first place. Ramon argued, in his review of social work in Slovenia, that social pedagogy is an integral part of Slovenian social work and can be characterised as being used either to 'promote social conformity *or* to promote self-directed learning which allows the person to be empowered as well as to take a critical stance on oneself and one's social context' (Ramon, 1995).

Employer driven social care – who is social care for?

On the face of it there appears to be little wrong with employers driving social care services. They control the resources and are often statutorily responsible for the legislative framework within which much social care practice takes place. The government departments responsible for social care have often seen employers as the keys to the delivery of social work services. In 2005 the Department of Health suggested that social work faced a number of challenges:

- Risk – the balance between enabling people to have control over their lives and ensuring they are safe.
- Information – people need information if they are to take responsibility for the situations they find themselves in. People need to be at the centre of assessing their own needs and how those needs can best be met.
- Direct payments – which can give people choice and control over the services they use and how they access them. Individual budgets will in this context be available for all adults with an assessed need.
- Personalised budgets – held by the local authority on behalf of the person using services or their carer.

Took, 2005, in Hatton, 2008

These challenges predated the recent inquiries and appeared to offer the hope of a more person centred, individually delivered, social work services. However, they are underpinned by an individualist philosophy which is consistent with a very managerial view of the social work task. They can be seen to individualise the relationship between the user/carer and welfare agencies thus promoting a narrow neo–liberal agenda rather than the more collectivist vision which many social work users, professionals and activists have argued for (Ferguson and Woodward, 2009; Barnes, 2007; see also the work of the Social Work Action Network). This is not to deny that such initiatives have the potential to secure real improvements to the lives of people using social work services but it does raise the issue of who controls these developments. Barnes has suggested that 'the main self determination issues for disabled people is not simply about service delivery mechanisms, but about whether levels of resources are sufficient to deliver the required services' (Barnes, 2007: 26). This comment applies equally to other areas of service delivery.

There is a need to recognise some deficiencies in UK social work and social care with its focus on managerial imperatives (Ferguson and Woodward, 2009 – see also this book's introduction). Ferguson and Woodward point to the work of Chris Jones who, they say, in researching the views of social practitioners 'discovered a depressing pattern, staff experiencing physical and emotional exhaustion, stress, frustration and resentment' (p. 49). While this is a consequence of neo-liberal policies which have individualised social work practice and compartmentalised the needs of people using social care and social work services, at least as important has been the deskilling of social workers' daily activities so that many of the aspirations that they held when coming into the job – to build good relationships with people using the services, to engage critically with practice, to seek to empower themselves and the people they work with – have become lost (Munro, 2010).

The issue of resources is high on the priorities of many social workers. Will the College of Social Work help to promote social work and through this deliver these resources? In the context of the severe cuts in welfare expenditure imposed as part of the current government's austerity measures this must be open to doubt. Indeed, the profession now faces further challenges:

- Public concern over what social workers do, reinforced by severe misrepresentation of the role of social workers by the media.
- Arguments that Higher Education Institutions fail to adequately train social workers, issues of 'preparedness for practice' and an unfair expectation and focus on newly qualified social workers. (Interestingly even the General Social Care Council recognised the unfairness of asking newly qualified social workers to take on 'complex assessment and safeguarding work' (GSCC, 2009: para 43). The challenge facing social work was reinforced by a senior manager from a local authority speaking at the Social Work Futures Conference held in the South of England when she said that at present approximately half of her child protection team was made up of newly qualified social workers.
- Recognition of the need to reconnect social workers to users/carers through prioritising face to face contact.

In all cases the solutions to these problems are often seen as procedural rather than systemic. The concern is with managing social work (both workers and people who use services) rather than transforming people's lives (Ferguson and Woodward, 2009; Hatton, 2008; Munro, 2011).

This creates tensions within social care and work. The tragedies where children die (which remain rare) are often used to legitimise expanding the regulatory framework rather than the enabling focus of the work social workers undertake. The move toward risk management or risk aversion rather than risk promotion, which the evidence suggests is the best way to facilitate the empowerment and development of the people we work with, is a case in point (Hatton, 2008; also see *Care Matters, Independence, Well being and choice* and *Our Health, Our care, Our say* for examples of how people who use services want the opportunity to take the same risks as their peers). This is occurring at a time when social work should be seeking to reconfigure the profession to make it more accountable and accessible. As a profession social work should be seeking to move to increase the amount of direct work it undertakes, to negotiate the space and freedom to undertake innovative, inclusive and radical interventions.

Social care and social work should be more widely defined as professional activities whose focus is on promoting societal improvement and change (in line with the IFSW definition of social work) and not as a means of managing the disadvantaged and excluded. *Protection* will always be a key part of the work of social workers' responsibilities but *prevention* and the *promotion of social justice* should again be put at the centre of all social care and social work interventions. This links with the conception of social pedagogy outlined in this book.

As Hämäläinen (2003) notes, 'social help has been radicalised' and he draws parallels with the move toward structural understandings and solutions similar to the development of radical social work in the UK (Hatton, 2001a, 2008). Such a re-conceptualisation can be assisted by social care and social work incorporating a social pedagogic paradigm into their current and future practice. In earlier chapters we have seen how a social pedagogic approach can fit with developing agendas in children's services (particularly residential services but also across the children's sector in line with the *Reclaiming Social Work* approach), adult services, youth work and community development. Social pedagogy's emphasis on the importance of direct work and its focus on the importance of relationships in good practice can enable it to make a real contribution to the practice of social work. The *CRISP* model, refracted through an understanding of power relationships, can be part of the process of revitalising social care and social work which many social workers anticipate as the outcome the new Professional Capability Framework being developed.

Summary

This chapter has looked at recent developments in UK social work following the deaths of Victoria Climbié and Baby Peter. The resulting reappraisal of social work exemplified by the *Social Work Task Force*, *Social Work Reform Board* and the *Munro Review of Child Protection* provides an opportunity to review contemporary developments in social work, and draws attention to the way existing practice had become overly procedural, risk averse and focused on managerial discourses. The chapter has argued that social pedagogy with its focus on relationships and inclusion can help transform current practice.

Exercise

Social work has been characterised as being too managerial and procedural. Can social pedagogy contribute to a reimagining of social work and if so, in what way?

Chapter 12: A UK Social Pedagogy?

While social professional work internationally shares many key characteristics it would be a mistake to simply try to transpose a particular model from one national context to another. The key to implementing social pedagogy in the UK is to develop an approach which draws on best practice but which is designed to meet the challenges of UK social welfare services. Looking at the potential efficacy of social pedagogy to children's residential services in the UK, CPEA suggested that:

> *The underlying principles of social pedagogy resonate with many of the current developments taking place within England e.g. in relation to developing a more holistic approach to work with children and young people and integrated working.*

CPEA, 2007: 33

Jackson, writing about the experience of using social pedagogic approaches in Scotland says:

> *An acceptance of a social pedagogic approach would necessitate not only a radical transformation in the character of residential care but also fundamental changes in the nature and purpose of professional training for those working in child care services.*

It is worth remembering however the multi-dimensional nature of the oppression faced by many people who use welfare services (Thompson, 2007; Dominelli, 2007). We have seen earlier in the book how social pedagogy as an approach resonates with progressive developments in a range of sectors not just the narrowly focused interventions around young people in public care with which much of the UK debate has become synonymous. It is worth remembering that this multi-dimensionality occurs across the personal, cultural and structural dimensions of people's experience (Thompson, 2009) or the micro, mezzo or macro levels (Hatton, 2008). Vaisanen (2010), a Finnish social pedagogue, suggests that within these spheres we need to give attention to the importance of the socio-cultural dimension. He suggests that there are four categories of intervention for the pedagogue at this level: a focus on the environment in which people are raised; a recognition of the importance of cultural engagement and activity; the promotion of involvement in recreational activities; and finally engagement with social activities. Underpinning this is a role for the social professional as 'an expert in the social potential of the young people' (p. 30) or in the case of this book, the wider community with whom we work.

Implementing social pedagogy in the UK therefore presents us with a double challenge of *Remembering* and *Refocussing*. *Remembering* because social and community work needs to retain a radical and campaigning aspect of our own practice, to reconnect with and remember the radical tradition and reclaim writers/activists such as Freire, Gramsci, and Fanon. However we also need to *Refocus*. Lorenz argues that:

> *Without a thorough systematic theoretical reflection on the relationship between interpersonal processes and social policy structures (the) sector will not only fail to formally professionalize but fail to deliver an accountable public service that renders people not only autonomous, but secures their social and citizenship rights.*

Lorenz, 2008: 641

This suggests the need to develop our understanding of the potential of social pedagogy and will require us to develop a more critical attitude toward future developments.

Theoretical engagement and praxis

A means of achieving this is to draw on ideas around structuration theory and the work of Foucault to reposit a link between agency and structure. Although largely discredited by the left for his writings on the Third Way, Gidden's earlier writings suggest a way in which we can move beyond a reliance on either structural or individualistic approaches to welfare practice. He writes about the relationship between agency and structure, referring to power as 'the transformative capacity of human action' (Cassell, 1993: 109). This, he suggests, following Marx, is the key element in the notion of praxis or the ability to link theory to practice. The creation of a radical practice, based on notions of overcoming oppression, tackling discrimination/oppression and the creation of new cooperative social relationships, is at the heart of any theory of social action. Bourdieu (2005) quotes appreciatively from Leach who railed against the belief that our options are limited by the structural constraints we face. Leach said, 'I postulate that structural systems in which all avenues of social action are narrowly institutionalised are impossible. In all viable systems, there must be an area where the individual is free to make choices, so as to manipulate the system to his advantage' (Leach, 1962: 133, in Bourdieu, 2005: 53).

So, what does this mean for us as social professionals? We need to engage with theory to generate an understanding of the world around us, so that we can use this 'consciousness' to implement social change (Freire, 1972). The focus for us as social professionals should therefore be on establishing the link between oppressive structures and individual action. These processes are essentially dialectical in that if we pursue change only at one level we will create either a nihilistic individualism or an authoritarian social order. Instead we need to engage in a process similar to that which Lefebrve described when discussing the Marxist concept of alienation: 'a specific alienation can be clearly defined only with reference to a possible disalienation, i.e. by showing how it can be overcome actually, by what practical means. The worst alienation is the blocking up of development' (Lefebrve, 1972: 9). To rephrase for our analysis, oppression can be understood by looking at how people become empowered and liberated.

Allman argues that Marx's concept of 'consciousness – in fact a theory of praxis . . . was revolutionary because it established the dialectical unity between our sensual experience of life and our thinking or consciousness' (Allman, 1999: 65). More importantly, it is a process which is transcendent in that it involves 'moving beyond' creating a new form of social relationship (Lefebrve, 1972). It is through working with people to unmask the structures of power and oppression, and to make explicit the processes through which they become rendered disempowered, that a more reflective and collective response can be developed, which aims to overcome the isolation and individualisation of the people with whom we work.

Foucault (1980: 142) pointed to the way in which power is localised, 'dispersed, heteromorphous' and accompanied by 'numerous phenomena, of inertia, displacement and resistance', so that 'one should not assume a massive and primal condition of domination, a binary structure with 'dominators' on the one side and 'dominated' on the other'. In fact, power should be viewed as a dynamic concept in which individuals 'are always in the position of simultaneously undergoing and exercising . . . power (they) are the vehicles of power, not its application' (p. 98). We need to create a 'reverse discourse' (Weedon, 1987; – see Chapter 5) in which instead of the social work agenda being set by the powerful we explicitly develop forms of practice which offer alternative forms of welfare practice.

Foucault (1980: 106) also suggested that 'the mechanisms of power (need to be analysed) on the basis of daily struggles at grass roots level, among those whose fight was located in the fine meshes of the web of power' (p. 116). In this, he argues, there is a role for what he calls *specific intellectuals.* Such specific intellectuals:

> . . . *encounter obstacles and face real dangers – the danger of remaining at the level of the conjunctural struggles, pressing demands restricted to particular sectors . . . above all the risk of being unable to develop these struggles for lack of a global strategy or outside support.*

> (p. 130)

As social professionals we need to see the larger picture, to be able to envisage alternatives which allow us to progress the humanistic agenda which lead most of us into social professional activity. This means that we should grasp the opportunity, which the very public focus on such work found in current debates around social professional practice outlined throughout this book provides. This will allow us to develop an approach to welfare practice work which moves beyond current preoccupations with risk aversion or at best risk management, to create a new vision for our work. This vision can be developed if we include within it the focus on inclusion, community, and relationships mentioned earlier. We need to create or recreate forms of intervention which emphasise human capacity, which promote fulfilling relationships and which at the same time seek to challenge current social structures which pathologise those using services and which focus on lack of capacity rather than human potential.

Summary

This chapter has argued for the relevance of social pedagogy to contemporary social professional practice in the UK. To maximise the potential of such an approach it has suggested the need to link theoretical engagement to practice.

Exercise

Is social pedagogy transferrable to the UK? If so, what are its implications for the work of social workers, youth workers, community workers and other social professions?

Part Five: Conclusion

Structural Social Pedagogy

How then can we see the future of social pedagogy in the UK? The earlier chapters suggest a need to generate a philosophical and organisational commitment to change. They also allow us to see the potential of introducing social pedagogy into a much wider range of settings. For good reasons the UK has largely looked at introducing social pedagogy into children's residential services. We have seen that this has had mixed results and the danger is that this will dissuade people from attempting to introduce it in to other contexts. This book has sought to demonstrate the potential for social pedagogic approaches to influence a wider range of social practices beyond residential child care, to youth work, community development and as part of the adult care and personalisation agenda. This is not to forget the potential of social pedagogy to refocus social work in the light of criticisms of its focus on proceduralism and managerialism discussed earlier.

This refocussing will involve us generating ideas which prevent social damage, promote human relationships and protect those who, for whatever reason, face marginalisation, exclusion and in some cases danger. To achieve this we do not need to extend the regulatory framework within which we operate but instead seek to create a new framework for our work which allows us to intervene where necessary but which is predicated on a positive view of human nature. Tragic events like the deaths of young children demonstrate the need for a highly motivated and skilled set of social professions. This is not the time to be further reducing professional discretion and further proceduralising practice. Social work, social care, youth work and community development if they are to gain public favour need to show that they can manage the tension between protection and empowerment.

To achieve this goal we need to reframe our practice or perhaps develop new forms of professional identity. We need to integrate social pedagogy, inclusion and community perspectives to refocus social work. As Smith and Whyte suggest social pedagogy can assist in the process of reframing through its concern with social justice (Smith and Whyte, 2008). This can be accomplished by taking up Lorenz's challenge to bring together interpersonal processes and social policy structures. A means of achieving this is to move beyond the relatively limited view of social pedagogy which is being hesitantly introduced into the UK, to recognise that social pedagogy is also capable of a radical reframing (in the UK context, if not the European one) so that it provides, in the words of Marynowicz-Hetka, 'an orientation for social action in the field of social practice' (2007: 1). As noted earlier it can in the right, supportive context improve inter-professional practice (Vrouwenfelder, Milligan and Merrell, 2012). Clearly such an approach is implied in the discussions of personalisation and community development in earlier chapters.

A possible solution is the development of a *structural social pedagogy* which integrates the humanistic, interpersonal, inclusive and relationship based focus of social pedagogy as currently put forward in the UK with a more radical vision which recognises the importance of using partnerships with service users to empower people to take control of the services on which they depend. Such an approach would be concerned with understanding and challenging the way social work is constructed as an activity which manages the poor. It would challenge the individualisation of users and recognise the structural element to relationships and particularly power relationships. Finally it would allow us to develop models of practice based on participation, inclusion, community and a commitment to social change.

Parton has said that we practice in a world which has become 'disoriented, disturbed and subject to doubt' (2003: 7) and that we need to engage in a process of reconstruction of social work (Parton and O'Byrne, 2000; Parton, 2003). *Structural social pedagogy* provides a way of achieving this. The 'common third' shows how we can mutually construct an alternative future, and a structuralist approach shows how we can engage in a social change agenda. This provides a major challenge for social professionals but one which will allow us to put forward a clear and consistent vision which makes our work distinctive from other forms of welfare practice and which will provide a way of resisting the neo-liberal paradigm we risk being constrained within.

A final illustration may point to the way in which we can incorporate social pedagogy into social professional practice. When speaking to the students who trained in social pedagogy and experienced UK social work I asked them to reflect on the relevance of social pedagogy to the UK. One of the students, Kristina, said:

> *I believe that the social pedagogic approach can be applied everywhere because it is a person-centered approach. If we really take interest in our users the approach is a helpful tool to challenge ourselves in ways of relating and in changing our own mindset so that we see the people we work with as equal, treat them with respect and love and by that create a fundament on which they can develop. In my dissertation I combined the 'common third' with anti-discriminatory practice and I really believe that the combination is giving the UK what you miss in theory and Denmark what we miss in theory . . . maybe I am being really naïve . . . I use that combination then I try to understand the children and their parents so that I am not limited to only the personal level . . . We need*

to know that we educate the children to take part in, and as a kindergarten in Denmark we need to teach them to take part in, the Danish society, school, democracy and a diversity of people. At the same time it is important that we understand what they come from so that we can tackle cultural and structural discrimination . . . the UK wants to empower and pedagogy is doing that on the personal level, if the professional is committed and possesses the values of equality, respect and dialog.

Kristina's analysis suggests that social pedagogy could be integrated into UK welfare practice and that we could benefit by learning from other countries' focus on equality and combining it with our commitment to diversity and difference. As I have noted elsewhere:

This process (of valuing other countries' perspectives) may allow us to see the similarities as well as the differences between us, to recognise that the truth does not reside in one set of culturally specific values but that ways of understanding, methods of working and commitments to social justice are often shared. Our countries may be at different stages, our experience is undoubtedly different but it may be found that what they have in common allows us to transcend any differences and work co-operatively toward a fairer future.

Hatton, 2001a: 276

Guide to Further Reading

This is an introductory text so it does not claim to present the final word on social pedagogy. It outlines some of the key concepts within social pedagogy and attempts to outline the beginnings of a conceptualisation of social pedagogy which is relevant to welfare practice in the UK. It is therefore something of a hybrid – providing a background to social pedagogy's introduction to the UK, outlining some key concepts from within the tradition, introducing what the author regards as a new conceptualisation of social pedagogy which integrates European and UK social work traditions and suggesting ways in which social pedagogy can be adopted to a wider field of practice than those in which it is currently considered in the UK.

Social pedagogy

A good starting point is the work of the Thomas Coram Research Unit at the Institute of Education. In particular it is worth reading the following:

Cameron, C. (2006) *New Ways of Educating: Pedagogy and Children's Services.* Final report to the Esmee Fairbairn Foundation. London: Thomas Coram Research Unit.

Cameron, C., McQuail, S. and Petrie, P. (2007*) Implementing the Social Pedagogic Approach For Workforce Training and Education in England: A Preliminary Study.* London: Thomas Coram Research Unit, University of London/Cabinet Office/ Department for Education and Skills.

Cameron, C. et al. (2010) *Implementing the DCSF Pilot Programme: The Work of The First Year.* Social Pedagogy Briefing Paper II. London: Thomas Coram Research Unit, Institute of Education, University of London.

Petrie, P. et al. (2006) *Working with Children in Care: European Perspectives.* Maidenhead: Open University Press.

Also worth looking at is the report of the Social Education Trust:

Bengtsson, E., Chamberlain, C., Crimmens, D. & Stanley, J. (2008) *Introducing Social Pedagogy into Residential Child Care in England: an Evaluation of a Project Commissioned by the Social Education Trust (SET) in September 2006 and Managed by the National Centre for Excellence in Residential Care (NCERRC).* London: SET/NCERRC.

To get a wider perspective on the range of interventions which social pedagogues engage in it is worth looking at two international collections:

Gustavsson, A., Hermannsson, H-E. & Hämäläinen, J. (2003) *Perspectives and Theory in Social Pedagogy.* Goteborg: Bokforlaget Daidalos.

Kornbeck, J. and Rosendal Jensen, N. (Eds.) (2009) *The Diversity of Social Pedagogy in Europe.* Bremen: Europaischer Hochschulverlag.

A recent addition is:

Cameron, C. and Moss, P. (Eds.) *Social Pedagogy and Working with Children and Young People.* London: Jessica Kingsley.

Two European writers who have looked at the implications of social pedagogy in the UK are Kornbeck (2002) and Hämäläinen (2003).

A definition of the competencies required of social educators and social pedagogues can be found in:

AIEJI (2009). *The professional competences of social educators: a conceptual framework* (available from http://www.aieji2009.dk/Background/media/aeiji/Professional%20competenc es%20of%20social%20educators.ashx – downloaded 02/05/2010) provides an outline of the competences required for social pedagogic/ social educational work and provides a useful counterpoint to the UK's National Occupational standards and the forthcoming *Professional Accountability Framework* (Social Work Reform Board, 2010).

Hatton, K. (2006, 2008, 2011) discusses the way in which social pedagogy can be adapted to the UK.

Creativity is a key concept in social pedagogy and it is worth looking at the collection of papers in the Spring 2009 edition of *Homeless in Europe*, the journal of FEANTSA, the European Federation of National Organisations Working with the Homeless, which looks at a wide range of projects using creative and artistic methods to involve homeless people. Although not citing social pedagogy as an approach they adopt, the methods used are consistent with a social pedagogic approach. At a UK level the social work programmes at the University of Portsmouth are underpinned by a social pedagogic approach. The programmes are delivered through a strong partnership with a service user/carer organisation the Social Work Inclusion Group (SWIG). SWIG has its own website which collects together a range of creative artefacts produced by the group, staff and students at the University. The website can be found at swig.org.uk. See also Dillon, L. (2010) *Looked After Children: An Evidence Review*, London: Youth Music.

It is also worth looking at websites of the Social Pedagogy Network and the National Children's Bureau for examples of creative approaches to pedagogy

Inclusion is another important concept if we are to articulate a conception of social pedagogy which connects with welfare developments in the UK. A good discussion of inclusion and its relevance to the UK can be found in Hatton (2008). Central to debates around inclusion are the ideas of power and empowerment. A good introduction to these concepts is Neil Thompson's *Power and Empowerment* (2007), and *Empowerment, Participation and Social Work* (2008) by Robert Adams. Lukes (2005) is an update of a classic text, and it is worth reading Foucault (1980) for a sophisticated analysis of the dispersed and fragmented nature of power.

Personalisation represents a significant development in the way adult social care is delivered. Some see it as creeping privatisation in which the state cedes its responsibility for providing welfare and places that responsibility on the individual. The author suggests that to resist this process it is worth reclaiming personalisation for a new form of intervention which is inclusive and supports the individual to meet their needs in partnership with welfare professionals. Drawing on some recent policy papers the author suggests that social pedagogy can provide such a vision. The key papers discussed are:

AIEJI (2010) *Working with Persons with Developmental Disabilities: The Role of the Social Educator.* Denmark, International Association of Social Educators (AIEJI) downloaded on 14/11/12 from aieji.net/wp-content/uploads/2010/12/working-with-persons-with-develo pmental-disbilities.pdf

Carter, S. et al. (2012) *Never Mind What I Like, It's Who I am That Matters: An Investigation Into Social Pedagogy as a Method to Enhance The Involvement of Young People With Learning Difficulties. British Journal of Learning Difficulties*, advance access downloaded 10/11/12

Department of Health (2009) *Working to Put People First: The Strategy for the Adult Social Care Workforce in England.* available at http://www.dh.gov.uk/publications downloaded 29/04/11

HM Government (2007) *Putting People First.* London: HMSO.

Local Authority Circular (2008) *Transforming Adult Social Care.* DoH.

Ramsden, S. (2010) *Practical Approaches to Co-Production.* London: DoH.

For a good account of the development of the personalisation agenda, Carr, S. (2010) *Personalistion: A Rough Guide.* London: Social Care Institute of Excellence.

Social pedagogy education in the UK

There are a number of courses in the UK which either offer a qualification in social pedagogy or utilise social pedagogy within other programmes. These include:

BA (Hons) in Social Pedagogy (formerly the BA (Hons) Curative Education (from 2003–2010) University of Aberdeen and the Camphill Rudholf Steiner School – see Jackson (2006).

BA (Hons) Social Pedagogy and Social Care, Liverpool Hope University (closing in July 2013).

BA (Hons) Applied Social Studies, Robert Gordon University (students can exit with a MA Social Pedagogy at the end of year three).

MA Social Pedagogy, Institute of Education, University of London.

Also the social work courses at the University of Portsmouth are underpinned by teaching on social pedagogy. This continues an earlier commitment to social pedagogy described in Hatton (2006).

Useful websites

AEIJI www.aeiji

ECCE European Centre for Community Education http://www.ecce-net.eu

ENSACT European Network for Social Action http://www.ensact.eu

FEANTSA www.feantsa.org

FESET www.feset.org

Jacaranda www.jacaranda-recruitment.co.uk

National Children's Bureau www.ncb.org.uk

Social Pedagogy Development Network www.social-pedagogy.co.uk

Thempra www.thempra.com

YouthMusic www.youthmusic.org.uk

Some Important Organisations and Contact Details

AIEJI – A statement about the competencies expected of social educators can be found at http://www.aieji2009.dk/Background/media/aeiji/Professional%20compet-enc es%20of%20social%20educators.ash

The purpose of AIEJI is to emphasise and promote the philosophy of social education and its uniqueness in being actively involved in partnership with clients, working with them, not only individually but in groups, families, communities and the social environments towards the development of their strengths and in resolving personal, social, and community difficulties.

ECCE – The European Centre for Community Education (ECCE) was founded on December, 15, 1985, in Oberwesel (Germany). ECCE has the legal form of a registered association.

Aims:

The fundamental task of the ECCE is to further the concept of Europe as a social community through the promotion of activities which will facilitate the comparison of existing models, and the possible development of new models of community education. In this context the term community education is used to include the fields of social work, community work, youth work, work with disadvantaged people and other related educational activities.

The Centre therefore is intended to promote greater knowledge and better understanding of different cultures amongst young people with particular reference to Europe, through providing educational experiences and training activities on a multilateral basis.

Objectives:

- To initiate, develop and promote multilateral exchanges.
- To provide intercultural learning opportunities for workers and for those engaged in their education and training in the field of community education.
- To develop networks for the exchange of information and research about theory and practice in the field of community education.

The ECCE is registered by the 'Amtsgericht Koblenz' (No. 2703) and recognised as a non-profit-making association by the 'Finanzamt Koblenz' (No. 22.7255-XI/6).

ENSACT – European Network for Social Action http://www.ensact.eu

ENSACT consists of six European Associations:

- European Association of Schools of Social Work (EASSW)
- Formation d'Educateurs Sociaux Européens / European Social Educator Training (FESET)
- Fédération Internationale des Communautés Educatives (FICE)
- International Association of Social Educators (AIEJI)
- International Council on Social Welfare European Region (ICSW)
- International Federation of Social Workers European Region (IFSW)

FEANTSA – The European Federation of National Organisations Working with the Homeless: http://www.feantsa.org

FESET – Association Européens des Comtes de Formation au Travail Socio-Educatif/ European Social Educator Training is a European association of training centres for socio-educational care work. www.feset.org
Aims:
According to the statutes, the aims of FESET are, whilst respecting the complete autonomy of the affiliated training centres:

- To promote the education and training for socio-educational purposes.
- To participate in programmes of different European bodies.
- To ensure that the training centres be represented at the institutions of the European Union, the Council of Europe as well as other international organisations.
- To encourage exchanges and understanding between training centres in the member states of the EU, in the member states of the Council of Europe and in other European states.
- To promote terms of mutual recognition of diplomas.

These aims have been further developed as follows:

- To be involved in European and International organisations as an NGO.
- To produce and sustain research and studies on the problems posed by the European Union understood merely as a free marketing of goods (social and economic impoverishment, exclusion and social injustice).
- To collaborate with other associations with similar goals.
- To support democratic and non-violent pedagogical methods enabling the full development of the individual as well as the highest degree of autonomy and social integration.
- To work in each European country for the enactment and development of social laws respecting the human rights of individuals with whom social pedagogues work as well as the rights and duties of the social pedagogues.

- To work in each European country for the development and professional regulation of socio-educational care work.
- To work for the development of the European dimension of socio-educational care work, including the de jure and de facto recognition of the profession itself.
- To promote and develop exchanges among the members of FESET in order to arrive at academic recognition of qualifications obtained in the member-schools.

IASSW – International Association of Schools of Social Work, www.iassw-aiets.org
See also the IASSW journal *Social Dialogue* at www.social-dialogue.com

Journal of Social intervention: Theory and Practice http://www.journalsi.org

SOCMAG – *The Social Work & Society Online News Magazine* (SocMag): www.socmag.net

SPDN – Social Pedagogy Development Network, www.thempra.org.uk

SWAN – The Social Work Action Network is a radical, campaigning organisation of social work and social care practitioners, students, service users, carers and academics, united by their concern that social work practice is being undermined by managerialism and marketisation, by the stigmatisation of service users and by welfare cuts and restrictions. While recognizing that social work is one of the mechanisms through which the State controls the behaviours of poor families, SWAN believes nevertheless that social work is a valuable activity which can help people address the problems and difficulties in their lives. Many of these difficulties are rooted in the inequalities and oppressions of the modern world and good social work necessarily involves confronting the structural and public causes of so many private ills. http://www.socialworkfuture.org

References

Aabro, C. (2004) *The Common Third*. Written correspondence with author.

AIEJI (2009) *The Professional Competences of Social Educators: A Conceptual Framework*. downloaded 02/05/2010) from http://www.aieji2009.dk/Background/media/aeiji/Professional%20competenc es%20 of%20social%20educators.ashx

AIEJI (2010) *Working with Persons with Developmental Disabilities: The Role of the Social Educator*. Denmark: International Association of Social Educators (AIEJI) downloaded on 14/11/12 from aieji.net/ wp-content/uploads/2010/12/working-with-persons-with-develo pmental-disbilities.pdf

Akcelrud Durao, F. (2006) Towards a Model of Inclusive Exclusion: Marginal Subjectivation in Rio de Janeiro. *A Contra corriente, A Journal of Social History and Literature in Latin America*, 3: 2, 88–106.

Allman, P. (1999) *Revolutionary Social Transformation: Democratic Hopes, Political Possibilities and Critical Education*. USA: Bergin and Garvey.

Aluffi-Pentini, A. and Lorenz, W. (1996) *Anti-racist Work with Young People*. Dorset: Russell House Publishing

Andersen, B. (2011) Commentary: International Cooperation between Social Pedagogues. *Child and Youth Services*, 32: 6–8.

Barnes, C. (2007) Disability Activism and the Price of Success: A British Experience. *Intersticios, Revista Sociologica de Pensamiento Critico*, 1: 2, 15–29.

Bateman, N. (2006) *Practising Welfare Rights*. London: Routledge.

Bengtsson, E. et al. (2008) *Introducing Social Pedagogy into Residential Child Care in England: An Evaluation of a Project Commissioned by the Social Education Trust (SET) in September 2006 and Managed by The National Centre For Excellence in Residential Care (NCERRC)*. London: SET/NCERRC.

Beresford, P. and Hoban, M. (2005) *Participation in Anti-Poverty and Regeneration Work and Research: Overcoming Barriers and Creating Opportunities*. York: Joseph Rowntree Foundation.

Berger, P. and Luckmann, T. (1971) *The Social Construction of Reality: A Treatise in the Sociology of Knowledge*. London: Penguin University Books.

Berridge, D. et al. (2011) *Raising the Bar? Evaluation of the Social Pedgogy Pilot Programme in Residential Children's Homes*. London: DfE.

Blackham, H.J. (1961) *Six Existentialist Thinkers*. London: Routledge and Kegan Paul.

Boddy, J. & Statham, J. (2009) *European Perspectives on Social Work: Models of Education and Professional Roles*. London: Thomas Coram Research Unit, Institute of Education.

Borghill, L. (2004) *The Empowerment of Young People at Risk Through Sport and Outdoor Activities*. unpublished undergraduate dissertation, University of Portsmouth.

Bourdieu, P. (2005) *The Logic of Practice*. Cambridge: Polity Press.

Boyce, N. (2010) *Social Pedagogy in Essex*. childrenwebmag (downloaded from www. childrenweb-mag.com/articles/social-pedagogy/social pedagogy in Essex on 25/10/12)

Cacinovic Vogrincic, G. (2005) Teaching Concepts of Help in Social Work: The Working Relationship. *European Journal of Social Work*, 8: 3, 335–41.

Cameron, C. (2004) Social Pedagogy and Care: Danish and German Practice in Young People's Residential Care. *Journal of Social Work*, 4: 2, 133–51.

Cameron, C. (2006) *New Ways of Educating: Pedagogy and Children's Services*. London: Thomas Coram Research Unit.

Cameron, C. and Moss, P. (2011) Social pedagogy: Current Understandings and Opportunities in Cameron,

C. and Moss, P. (2011) *Social Pedagogy and Working with Children and Young people: Where Care and Education Meet.* London: Jessicca Kingsley.

Cameron, C. and Petrie, P. (2011) *Social Pedagogy and Foster Care: A Scoping Paper to Inform the Fostering Network.* London: Thomas Coram Research Unit, Institute of Education, University of London.

Cameron, C., McQuail, S. and Petrie, P. (2007*) Implementing the Social Pedagogic Approach For Workforce Training and Education in England: A Preliminary Study.* London: Thomas Coram Research Unit, University of London/Cabinet Office/Department for Education and Skills.

Cameron, C. et al. (2011) *Final Report of the Social Pedagogy Pilot Project: Development and Implementation.* Thomas Coram Research Unit/Institute of Education, University of London.

Carr, S. (2010) *Personalistion: A Rough Guide.* London: Social Care Institute of Excellence.

Carter, S. et al. (2012) Never Mind What I Like, It's Who I am That Matters: An Investigation Into Social Pedagogy as a Method to Enhance The Involvement of Young People With Learning Difficulties. *British Journal of Learning Difficulties*, advance access downloaded 10/11/12.

Cassell, P. (1993) *The Giddens Reader.* Basingstoke: Macmillan.

Chambers, H. (2004) *Creative Arts and Play for the Well-Being of Looked After Children.* London: NCB.

Chambers, H. and Petrie, P. (2009) *A Learning Framework for Artist Pedagogues.* London: CCE and NCB.

Charles, M. and Wilson, J. (2004) Creativity and Constraint in Child Welfare. In Lymbery, M. and Butler, S. (Eds.) (2004) *Social Work Ideals and Practice Realities.* Basingstoke: Palgrave, Macmillan.

Clarke, J. and Cochrane, A. (1998) The Social Construction of Social Problems. In Saraga, E. (Ed.) *Embodying the Social: Constructions of Difference.* London: Routledge/ Open University.

Cole and Wertsch (1996) Beyond the Individual-Social Antinomy in Discussions of Piaget and Vygotsky. *Human Development*, 39, 250–6.

Coussee, F. et al. (2008) The Emerging Social Pedagogical Paradigm in UK Child and Youth Care: Deus ex Machina or Walking the Beating Path? *British Journal of Social Work*, 1–17.

CPEA (2007) *Social Pedagogy and The Young People's Workforce.* Liverpool: CPEA.

Craig, G. Gorman, M. & Vercseg, I. (2004) *The Budapest Declaration: Building European Civil Society Through Community Development.* International Association for Community Development, Combined European Bureau for Community Development, Hungarian Association for Community Development.

Davies Jones, H. (1986) The Profession at Work in Contemporary Society in Courtioux. In Davies Jones, M., Kalcher, H., Steinhauser, J., Tuggener, W. and Walldjik, H. (Eds.) *The Social Pedagogue in Europe – Living as a Profession.* Zurich: FICE (Federation Internationale des Communautes Educatives) with the support of UNESCO.

Davies Jones, H. (1994) The Social Pedagogues in Wester Europe: Some Implicatins for European Inter-professional Care. *Journal of InterProfessional Care*, 8: 1, 19–29.

DCSF (2008) *Children looked after in England ending 31 March 2007.* Retrieved 05/02/08 http://www.dcsf.gov.uk/rsgateway/DB/SFR/s000741/SFR27-2007rev.pdf

Department for Communities and Local Government (2006) *Strong and Prosperous Communities.* London: HMSO.

Department of Health (2008) *Transforming Adult Social Care.* London: DoH.

Department of Health (2009) *Working to Put People First: The Strategy for the Adult Social Care Workforce in England* available at http://www.dh.gov.uk/publications downloaded 29/04/11

Department of Health (2010) *A Vision for Adult Social Care: Capable Communities and Active Citizens.* London: HMSO.

DfES (2004) *Every Child Matters: Next Steps.* London: HMSO.

DfES (2007) Care Matters: Transforming the Lives of Children and Young People in Care. London: HMSO.

Eichsteller, G. and Holtoff, S. (2011) Conceptual Foundations of Social Pedagogy: A Transnational Perspective from Germany. In Cameron, C. and Moss, P. (Eds.) *Social Pedagogy and Working with Children and Young People*. London: Jessica Kingsley.

Eichsteller, G. and Rapey, D. (2006) *Social Pedagogy and Youth Work*. Paper presented at the conference organised by the Thomas Coram Research Unit, University of London December 2006.

Eriksson, L. (2011) Community Development and Social Pedagogy: Traditions For Understanding Mobilization For Collective Self Development. *Community Development Journal*, 46: 4, 403–20.

Eriksson, L. and Markstrom, A.M. (2003) Interpreting the Concept of Social Pedagogy. In Gustavsson, A. Hermansson, H.E. and Hamalainen, J. (Eds.) *Perspectives and Theory in Social Pedagogy*. Gotenburg: Bokforlaget Daidalos.

Fanon, F. (1978) *Black Skin, White Masks*. Harmondsworth: Penguin.

FEANTSA (2009) *Homeless in Europe*. Spring.

Ferguson, I. and Woodward, R. (2009) *Radical Social Work in Practice: Making a Difference*. Bristol: Policy Press.

Feuer, L.S. (Ed.) (1972) *Marx and Engels: Basic Writings on Politics and Philosophy*. London: Fontana.

Flanagan, C. Syvertsen, A. and Wray-Lake, L. (2007) Youth Political Activism: Sources of Public Hope in the Context of Globalisation. In Silbersian, R.K. and Lerner, R.M. *Approaches to Positive Youth Development*. London: Sage.

Fog, E. (2003) A Social Pedagogical Perspective on Milieu Therapy. In Gustavsson, A. Hermansson, H.E. and Hämäläinen, J. (Eds.) *Perspectives and Theory in Social Pedagogy*. Gotenburg: Bokforlaget Daidalos.

Fook, J. (2002) Theorizing From Practice: Towards an Inclusive Approach for Social Work. *Qualitative Social Work*, 1:1, 79–95.

Foucault, M. (1980) *Power/Knowledge: Selected Interviews and Other writings 1972–1977*. Gordon, C. (Ed.) London: Harvester Wheatsheaf.

Freire, P. (1972) *Pedagogy of the Oppressed*. Harmondsworth: Penguin.

Fremeaux, I. (2005) New Labour's Appropriation of The Concept of Community: A Critique. *Community Development Journal*, 40: 3, 265–74.

Gardiner, P. (1998) *Past Masters: Kierkegaard*. Oxford: Oxford University Press.

Gardner, A. (2011) *Personalisation in Social Work*. Exeter: Learning Matters.

General Social Care Council (2009) *Raising Standards: Social Work Education in England, 2007–8*. London: General Social Care Council.

Gray, M. & Webb, S.A. (2008) Debate: Social Work as Art Revisited. *International Journal of Social Welfare*, 17: 182–93.

Gulati, A. and King, A. (2009) *Supporting Vulnerable Young People in Transition*. Final report to Quartet Community Foundation For The West of England, Perspective UK.

Günther, K.H. (1993) Friedrich Adolph Wilhelm Diesterweg (1790–1866) downloaded 3/12/2012 from www.ibe.unesco.org/fileadmin/user . . . upload/archive/publication/ThinkersPDF/diestere.pdf

Gustavsson, A. Hermansson, H.E. and Hämäläinen, J. (Eds.) *Perspectives and Theory in Social Pedagogy*. Gotenburg: Bokforlaget Daidalos.

Hacking, S. et al. (2009) The Empowerment of People With Mental Health Needs and Other Social Exclusion Impacts Using Arts Participation: Evidence From The Uclan/Anglia Research Project. *Homeless in Europe*, Spring, 11–4.

Hämäläinen, J. (2003) The Concept of Social Pedagogy in The Field of Social Work. *Journal of Social Work*, 3: 1, 70–80.

Hannay, A. and Marino, G.D. (1998) *The Cambridge Companion to Kierkegaard*. Cambridge: Cambridge University Press.

Hatton, K. (2001a) Translating Values: Making Sense of Different Value Bases: Reflections From Denmark and the UK. *International Journal of Social Research Methodology*, 4: 4, 265–78.

Hatton, K. (2001b) *The Dialectics of Exclusion and Empowerment: An Examination of The Role of Social Professionals in Denmark, Ireland and the UK.* Unpublished PhD Thesis, University of Portsmouth.

Hatton, K. (2006) Europe and the Undergraduate Programme. in Lyons, K. and Lawrence, S. *Social Work in Europe: Educating For Change.* Birmingham: BASW/Venture Press.

Hatton, K. (2008) *New Directions in Social Work Practice.* Exeter: Learning Matters.

Hatton, K. (2011a) Changing Professional Identities: Towards a Structural Social Pedagogy. In Seibel, F.W. et al. (Eds.) *European Developments and The Social Professions.* Brno: Czech Republic, European Centre for Community Education.

Hatton, K. (2011b) *Creativity, Inclusion and Social Pedagogy.* Paper delivered to the Participatory Arts and Social Practices Conference in October.

Hatton, K. (2012a) Le travail communautaire au Royaume-Uni durant les annees 1970–1980 souvenirs d'un temps revolu? *Vie Sociale*, 2, 99–110.

Hatton. K. (2012b) Youth Inclusion and Social Pedagogy: A UK Perspective. *Biennale internationale l'education, de la formation et des pratiques professionnelles.*

Healy, K. (2008) Debate: Critical Commentary on 'Social Work as Art Revisited. *International Journal of Social Welfare*, 17: 194–5.

Hermansson, H.E. (2003) Social Economy, Social Pedagogy and New Forms of Work Within the Field of Disability. In Gustavsson, A., Hermansson, H.E. and Hämäläinen, J. (Eds.) *Perspectives and Theory in Social Pedagogy.* Gotenburg: Bokforlaget Daidalos.

Higham, P. (2001) Changing Practice and an Emerging Social Pedagogue Paradigm in England: the Role of the Personal Advisor. *Social Work in Europe*, 8: 1, 21–6.

Hinshelwood, R.D. (1978) *What's Happening in Groups.* London: Heinman.

Hinshelwood, R.D. (1989) *The Social Possession of Identity.* In Richards, B. *Crises of the Self.* London: Free Association Books.

HM Government (2007) *Putting People First.* London: HMSO.

House of Commons Children, Schools and Families Committee (2009) *Training of Children and Families Social Workers, Session 2008–9. Report, together with formal minutes.* London: HMSO.

http://www.dfes.gov.uk/consultations/downloadableDocs/6781-DfES-CM%20Summary.pdf   Retrieved17/02/08

Hurstel, L. (2012) The Banlieu in Europe. Paper presented at *Biennale internationale l'education, de la formation et des pratiques professionnelles*, Paris, France.

Jackson, R. (2003) The Spiritual Dimension in Child and Youth Care Work, *The International Child and Youth Care Network*, Issue 57. http://www.cyc-net.org/cyc-online/cycol–1003-spiritualneeds.html.

Jackson, R. (2006) The Role of Social Pedagogy in The Training of Residential Child Care Workers. *Journal of Intellectual Disabilities*, 10: 1, 61–73.

Jordan, B. (2006) *Social Policy For The Twenty-First Century.* Cambridge: Polity.

Jordan, B. (2007) *Social Work and Well-being.* Lyme Regis: Russell House Publishing.

Jordan, B. (2011) Making Sense of the 'Big Society': Social Work and the Model Order. *Journal of Social Work*, 1–7.

Kendall, K.A. (2000) *Social Work Education: Its origins in Europe.* Alexandria, VA: Council of Social Work Education.

Kornbeck, J. (2002) Reflections on The Exportability of Social Pedagogy and Its Possible Limits. *Social Work in Europe*, 9: 2, 37–49.

Kornbeck, J. & Rosendal Jensen, N. (2009) Introduction: Social Pedagogy in Europe – Diverse with Common Features. In Kornbeck, J. & Rosendal Jensen, N. (Eds.) *The Diversity of Social Pedagogy in Europe, Studies in Comparative Social Pedagogies and International Social Work, Vol VII*. Bremen: Europaischer Hochschulverlag.

Langager, S. (2009) Social Pedagogy and 'At-Risk' Youth: Societal Changes and New Challenges in Social Work With Youth. In Kornbeck, J. & Rosendal Jensen, N. (Eds.) *The Diversity of Social Pedagogy in Europe, Studies in Comparative Social Pedagogies and International Social Work, Vol VII*, Bremen: Europaischer Hochschulverlag.

Lefebrve, H. (1972) *The Sociology of Marx*. Harmondsworth: Penguin.

Lone, A. (2010) Collectives: A Norwegian Success Story in Residential Care For Drug Addicts Based on a Social Pedagogical Approach. *European Journal of Social Education*, 18/19: 60–72.

Lonie, D. (2011) *Looked After Children and Music Making*. Paper presented to School of Health Sciences and Social Work research seminar at the University of Portsmouth, April 13th.

Lord Laming (2009) *The Protection of Children in England: A Progress Report*. London: HMSO.

Lorenz, W. (1994) *Social Work in a Changing Europe*. London: Routledge.

Lorenz, W. (2008) Paradigms and Politics: Understanding Methods Paradigms in an Historical Context: The Case of Social Pedagogy. *British Journal of Social Work*, 38, 625–44.

Lukes, S. (1972) *Power: A Radical View*. Basingstoke: Macmillan Education.

Lymbery, M.E.F. (2009) Negotiating the Contradictions between Competence and Creativity in Social Work Education. *Journal of Social Work*, 3: 1, 99–117.

Lyons, K. (1999) *International Social Work: Themes and perspectives*. Aldershot: Ashgate.

Lyons, K. & Lawrence, S. (Eds.) (2006) *Social Work in Europe: Educating for Change*. Birmingham: IASSW/Venture Press.

Macquarrie, J. (1972) *Existentialism: An Introduction, Guide and Assessment*. London: Penguin.

Marynowicz-Hetka, E. (2007) Towards the Transversalism of Social Pedagogy. *Social Work and Society, International Online Journal*, 5: 3.

Marynowicz-Hetka, E., Piekarski, J. and Wagner, A. (1999) Issues in Social Work: An Invitation to a Discussion. In Marynowicz-Hetka, E., Piekarski, J., Wagner, and Katowice, A. (Eds.) *European Dimensions in Training and Practice of the Social Professions*, 'Slask' SP z o.o Wydawnictwo Naukowe.

Mayo, P. (1999) *Gramsci, Freire and Adult Education: Possibilities of Transformative Action*. Basingstoke: Macmillan.

McLaughlin, J. (1995) *Travellers and Ireland: Whose Country, Whose History?* Cork: Cork University Press.

McLaughlin, J. (1998) The Political Geography of Anti-Traveller Racism in Ireland: The Politics of Exclusion and The Geography of Closure. *Political Geography*, 17: 4, 417–35.

Memmi, A. (1990) *The Coloniser and the Colonised*. London: Earthscan.

Milligan, I. (2009) *Introducing Social Pedagogy into Scottish Residential Child Care: an Evaluation of the Sycamore Services Social Pedagogy Training Programme*. Glasgow: Scottish Institute for Residential Child Care/University of Strathclyde.

Milligan, I. and Stevens, I. (2006) *Residential Child Care: Collaborative Practice*. London: Sage.

Morison, J. (2000) Government-Voluntary Sector Compacts: Governance, Governmentality and Civil Society. *Journal of Law and Society*, 27: 1, 98–132.

Munro, E. (2011) *The Munro Review of Child Protection: Final Report*. London: HMSO.

National Children's Bureau (2005) *Healthy Care Briefing: Play and Creativity*. London: NCB.

National Youth Agency (2009) *Arts Work With Socially Excluded Young People*. Leicester: NYA.

Needham, C. and Carr, S. (2009) *Co-production: an Emerging Evidence Base For Adult Social Care Transformation*. London. Social Care Institute for Excellence.

Nordic Forum for Social Educators (2003) *Social Education and Social Educational Practice in the Nordic Countries.* Kopenhagen Nordisk Forum for Socialpadeagoger.

Okitikpi, T. and Aymer, C. (2008) *The Art of Social Work Practice.* Dorset: Russell House Publishing.

Ott, L. (2011) *Pédagogie sociale: Une pédagogie pour tous les éducateurs.* Lyon: Chronique Sociale.

Ott, L. (2012) *Relations parents/enfants.* Paper presented at Innovations Sociales et Territoires Conference, Montrouge, Paris Du 7 au 9 fevrier.

Oxtoby, K. (2009) *How Does Social Pedagogy Work on The Continent, and What are The Barriers to its Use in the UK. Lessons on Europe From Pedagogy.* Available from: http://www.communitycare.co.uk/articles/2009/03/18/111007/social-pedagogy-in-practice.html

Parton, N. (2003) Rethinking Professional Practice: The Contributions of Social Constructionism and the Feminist 'Ethics of Care'. *British Journal of Social Work*, 33, 1–16.

Parton, N. and O'Byrne, P. (2000) *Constructive Social Work: Towards a New Practice.* Basingstoke: Macmillan.

Payne, M. and Askeland, G.A. (2008) *Globalisation and International Social Work: Post-Modern Change and Challenge.* Aldershot: Ashgate.

Peacock, M. (2009) How The Arts Can Deliver Real Change For People. *Homeless in Europe*, Spring, 4–5.

Pecseli, B. (1996) *Kultur & Pedagogic*, Denmark, Munskaard, Rosinante.

Perkins, D.F., Borden, L.M. and Villarruel, F.A. (2001) Community Youth Development: A Partnership for Action. *The School Community Journal*, 11: 2, 39–56.

Petrie, P. (2001) The Potential of Pedagogy/Education for Work in the Children's Sector in the UK. *Social Work in Europe*, 8: 3, 23–5.

Petrie, P. (2002) The Potential of Pedagogy/Education for Work in the Children's Sector in the UK. *Social Work in Europe*, 8: 3, 23–5.

Petrie, P. and Chambers, H. (2009) *Richer Lives: Creative Activities in The Education and Practice of Danish Pedagogues, A Preliminary Study.* London: Thomas Coram Research Unit/Institute of Education, University of London.

Petrie, P. et al. (2006) *Working with Children in Care: European Perspectives.* Maidenhead: Open University Press.

Petrie, P. et al. (2009) *Pedagogy: A Holistic, Personal Approach to Work With Children and Young People, Across Sevices.* Briefing paper. London: Thomas Coram Research Unit/Institute of Education, University of London.

Purcell, P. (2012) Community Development and Everyday Life. *Community Development Journal*, 47: 2, 266–81.

Ramon, S. (1995) Slovenian Social Work: A Case Study of Unexpected Developments in the post – 1990 Period. *British Journal of Social Work*, 25, 513–28.

Ramsden, S. (2010) *Practical Approaches to Co-Production.* London: DoH.

Regional Youth Work Unit North East/ University of Sunderland (2010) *A Study on the Understanding of Social Pedagogy and its Potential Implications for Youth Work Practice and Training.* University of Sunderland.

Revera, N. (2001) The Role of the Personal Adviser: Some Observations on Social Pedagogy from the Netherlands. *Social Work in Europe*, 8: 1, 29–31.

Ruch, G., Turney, D. and Ward, A. (Eds.) (2010) *Relationship Based Social Work: Getting to the Heart of Practice.* London: Jessica Kingsley.

Scottish Executive (2005) *The Role of the Social Worker in the 21st Century: a Literature Review.* Edinburgh: Scottish Executive Education Department.

Shepherd, P. (2012) *Creative Resistance: Utilising Critical Theory and Service User Participation to Enhance*

Social Work Students' Ability to Deconstruct Visual Representations of 'Otherness'. Poster presentation at the Diversity in Education conference, 24/5th April, Whittlebury Hall, Conference Centre.

Smith, M.K. (2008a) *Froebel* (1782–1852) available at www.infed/org/thinkers/et-froeb.htm, downloaded on 16/10/2009.

Smith, M.K. (2008b) *Johann Heinrich Pestalozzi*. Infed, available at www.infed.org/thinkers/et-pest.htm downloaded on 14/12/12.

Smith, M. and Whyte, B. (2008) Social Education and Social Pedagogy: Reclaiming a Scottish Tradition in Social Work. *European Journal of Social Work*, 11: 1, 15–28.

Social Care Institute of Excellence (2004) *Involving Service Users and Carers in Social Work Education, Resource Guide No 2*. London: SCIE.

Social Work Task Force (2009) *Facing up to The Task: The Interim Report of the Social Work Task Force: July 2009*. London: DoH and DfCSF.

Stepney, P. and Popple, K. (2008) *Social Work and The Community: A Critical Context For Practice*. Basingstoke: Palgrave.

Swile, G.D. (2005) *Philosophical Foundations of Education*. Ohio: Pearson Merrill Prentice Hall.

Thompson, N. (2007) *Power and Empowerment*. Lyme Regis: Russell House Publishing.

Turner, L. (2007) *The Pedagogy of Che Guevara*. Havana: Editorial Capitan San Luis.

Turney, D., Ward, A. and Ruch, G. (2010) Conclusion. In Ruch, G., Turney, D. and Ward, A. (Eds.) *Relationship Based Social Work: Getting to the Heart of Practice*. London: Jessica Kingsley.

UK Race & Europe Network (UKREN) (2006) *Burning Cities: Lessons from the French Uprising for Europe and Britain Today*. London: UKREN secretariet, c/o Runnymede Trust.

UNICEF (2001) *The Participation Rights of Adolescents: A Strategic Approach*. New York: United Nation's Children's Fund.

United Nation's Children's Fund (2001) *The Participation Rights of Adolescents: A Strategic Approach*. New York: United Nations, Working Paper Series.

Vaisanen, R. (2010) Social Pedagogical Approach in Youth Social Work. *Journal Européen D'Education Sociale*, 18/19, 23–34.

Van Der Wende, M. (2001) The International Dimension in National Higher Education Politics: What Has Changed in Europe in The Last Five Years? *European Journal of Education*, 36: 4, 431–41.

Vrouwenfelder, E., Milligan, I. and Merrell, M. (2012) *Social Pedagogy and Inter-Professional Practice : Evaluation of Orkney Islands Training Programme*. Glasgow: University of Strathclyde.

Vygotsky, L. (1997) Interaction between Learning and Development. In Gauvin, M. and Cole, M. *Readings on the Development of Children*. 2nd edn, New York: WH Freeman.

Vygotsky, L. (2004) Imagination and Creativity in Childhood. *Journal of Russian and East European Psychology*, 42: 1, 7–97.

Weedon, C. (1987) *Feminist Practice and Post-structuralist Theory*. Oxford: Blackwell.

Yuval-Davis, N. (1998) Beyond Differences: Women, Empowerment and Coalition Politics. In Charles, N. and Hintjens, H. (Eds.) *Gender, Ethnicity and Political Ideologies*. London: Routledge.

Yuval-Davis, N. (2011) *Power, Intersectionality and the Politics of Belonging*. Aalborg: Feminist Research Centre.

Social work models, methods and theories
A framework for practice
Second edition

Edited by Paul Stepney and Deirdre Ford

'A very comprehensive book . . . seeks to challenge the reader or practitioner to take stock of the way that they practise and to view this in the wider context of both social policy and social inequalities and the impact that each has on practice and the impact that practice has on the individual . . . there are many highlights . . . of use to both the student and experienced practitioner. It is not just an exposition of theory but rather an aid to critical thinking of how and why we do what we do as practitioners.' Rostrum.

Contributors include Lena Dominelli, Peter Henriques, Bill Jordan, Malcolm Payne, Brian Sheldon and Pamela Trevithick.

2012. 978-1-905541-83-6.

Children's services at the crossroads
A critical evaluation of contemporary policy for practice

Edited by Patrick Ayre and Michael Preston-Shoot

'Challenging and thought-provoking.' Rostrum.

'A sustained academic critique . . . and a cri de coeur . . . It covers the period in which evidence-based practice has developed in the UK and presents an indictment of how the evidence base has sometimes been selectively used or ignored . . . We need less rhetoric, fewer initiatives, more listening, more focus on doing the job well, more respect and support for those on the child-care front line.' Research in Practice.

2010. 978-1-905541-64-5.

The barefoot helper
Mindfulness and creativity in social work and the helping professions

By Mark Hamer

'A refreshing discourse on regaining the soul of social work by becoming more authentic people ourselves . . . who knows, it could be the start of social work ridding itself of its corporate dullness and becoming the exciting, creative profession that seduced many of us in the first place.' Wellbeing.

'Might help you to do your job better, stay sane and be happy.' Addiction Today. 'I endorse it wholeheartedly.' The Guardian's barefoot doctor.

2006. 978-1-905541-03-4.